D1180572

0225 666 847 0 609 86

WESTMINSTER
CATHEDRAL
1895–1995

WESTMINSTER
CATHEDRAL
1895–1995

Peter Doyle

GEOFFREY
CHAPMAN

WEST GRID STAMP

NN		RR	5/95	WW	
NT		RT		WO	
NC		RC		WL	
NH		RB		WM	
NL		RP		WT	
NV		RS		WA	
NM		RW		WR	
NB		RV		WS	
NE					
NP					

Geoffrey Chapman

A Cassell imprint

Wellington House, 125 Strand, London WC2R 0BB
387 Park Avenue South, New York, NY 10016-8810

© Peter Doyle 1995

All rights reserved. No part of this publication may be reproduced or transmitted in any form or by any means, electronic or mechanical including photocopying, recording or any information storage or retrieval system, without prior permission in writing from the publishers.

First published 1995

British Library Cataloguing-in-Publication Data
A catalogue record for this book is available from the British Library.

ISBN 0-225-66684-7

Designed by John Leath, MSTD
and typeset in Stanley Morison's Times New Roman
with Eric Gill's Perpetua

A M D G

Typeset by Litho Link Ltd, Welshpool, Powys
Printed and bound in Great Britain by Biddles Ltd, Guildford & King's Lynn

For

BARBARA

MATTHEW *and* CATHERINE

Contents

Illustrations in text

Photographs

Introduction

WHEN I SET OUT to write the history of Westminster Cathedral over its first hundred years I had the idea of building it around three main themes: the Cathedral as a national flagship for English Catholicism, a national centre or focus; the Cathedral as a building of architectural merit in its own right, and the Cathedral as the centre of the diocese of Westminster and as a parish church. I wanted to avoid writing about it in isolation, and so I have tried to build into the story enough of what was happening to English Catholicism in those hundred years to provide a wider context.

The book is not a systematic history of the Cathedral – that would have required far more space than was available, and far more time. And those who are expert in such matters will soon realize that neither is it an exhaustive study of the architecture or of the music of the Cathedral. Important as both of these are in the story of the Cathedral, in addition to more space and time such a study would have called on specialist skills and knowledge which I do not possess.

I have enjoyed researching and writing the book and while doing so I have incurred many debts of gratitude which I would like to acknowledge here. The Diocesan Archivist, Fr Ian Dickie, has been extremely helpful and has given generously of his time and knowledge. A number of people have kindly given me time to interview them: His Eminence Cardinal Basil Hume; Bishop Gordon Wheeler; George Malcolm CBE, Fr Michael Hollings; Mgr David Norris; Mr Anthony Bartlett; Mgr George Stack, and Mr Peter Hannigan. The Cathedral often seems to cast a spell over those who work for or in it for any length of time, and it has been my pleasure to learn so much from these 'insiders'. Other people have been generous in their help and advice or in lending materials: Peter Howell of the Victorian Society; Cathal and Doreen O'Dwyer; Professor Tarn of the University of Liverpool; David Parsons and Joan Stephenson, and John MacGregor of the Cathedral Project Review Committee. Others have supported the idea of writing the book from the beginning: Fr John Arnold, Bishop P. O'Donoghue and Gemma Boase of the Friends of the Cathedral – the last of whom has worked hard to bring the original idea to fruition and has given both encouragement and a number of invaluable introductions.

I apologize to anyone whom I should have thanked and whose name I have omitted. I also apologize to the many people who devoted a large part of their lives to serving the Cathedral in one way or another over the century covered here and to whose memory I have not done justice.

Every effort has been made to trace the copyright of the photographs and drawings used as illustrations; it has not been an easy task, especially for materials from the early years.

Finally, and inadequately, a word of thanks to my wife and family to whom this book is lovingly dedicated and without whose support the task would have been well-nigh impossible; they have had to live under the shadow of St Edward's Tower for too long.

Peter Doyle

Bedford, February 1994

Chapter 1

A mixed legacy: English Catholics at the end of the nineteenth century

HERBERT VAUGHAN, founder of the Cathedral, became Archbishop of Westminster in April 1892. For twenty years before that he had been Bishop of Salford, the smallest of the English Catholic dioceses in area, though one of the most populous. He came from an old Catholic gentry family and was the eldest of thirteen children; six of the eight boys became priests and all five girls became nuns. In many ways he epitomized one of the important strands which made up English Catholicism in the nineteenth century: those recusant families which had kept the faith through the years of persecution, providing priests and nuns from their children, sometimes fulfilling the role of local gentry but rarely making an impact on the national scene. They were very English in their outlook despite being barred from many of the activities of their Protestant fellow countrymen. Part of Herbert Vaughan's education had been at a Jesuit college in Belgium (where he was apparently known as 'Milord Roastbeef') – another recusant tradition, carried on even when there was no longer any need for it. His mother had been a convert, in this representing another strand that was to enrich the English Catholic body. As Bishop of Salford he had proved himself a very able administrator, concerned with the plight of the poor Irish who constituted the majority of his people (and who were, of course, a third strand in the make-up of English Catholicism) and dedicated to making every provision possible for their religious welfare. Before becoming bishop he had founded a missionary congregation which was to spread throughout the world, the Mill Hill Missionaries. Such was the man who became third Archbishop of Westminster.[1]

1

What was the state of the English Catholic body which he took over from Cardinal Manning? It had grown in size in the fifty years since Nicholas Wiseman, the first Cardinal Archbishop of Westminster, had become its leader. Exact statistics are impossible to find, but a figure of 750,000 Catholics in England and Wales in 1850 seems a fair estimate. This more than doubled by 1900 to about 1.7 million, while over the same period the general population had increased by 81 per cent. The number of priests had been 788 in 1850; by 1900 this had risen to 3,000. Another way of assessing this increase is to say that in 1850 only one diocese out of thirteen had more than a hundred priests (two others had over ninety); by 1900 all but two had more than a hundred, and three dioceses had more than three hundred. The number of churches and chapels open to the public had been 587 in 1850 in England and Wales; this had increased to 1,500 by the end of the century. Church building was important not just in order to provide places for the increasing Catholic population: it was one sign of arrival, of ecclesiastical respectability in a church-building age. As a London priest had said of his new church in Commercial Road, the existence of a 'fine' church had doubled his congregation and raised it 'at least fifty years in social position and consideration'. From this point of view, Westminster Cathedral could be regarded as the final proof of Catholic ability to build well and expensively and so to keep up with one's Protestant neighbours; but it would be wrong to forget the other fine, and expensive, churches which had been erected up and down the country.[2]

Despite this growth England was still a missionary country in two respects. Technically, even though diocesan bishops had been established in 1850, the Catholic affairs of the country were under the control of the Roman Congregation for the Propagation of the Faith (Propaganda), which looked after missionary territories around the world. It was not until 1908 that the Roman authorities considered the English Catholic Church to be mature enough to be allowed to drop its missionary status. And in reality, much of England and Wales was missionary territory. Outside the large urban centres, and a few traditionally Catholic rural areas, anything resembling a Catholic presence was non-existent. This was particularly true of large parts of Wales and of the dioceses of Plymouth, Clifton and Northampton. The latter was the largest in area, covering seven counties and stretching from the Wash to the Thames. In 1851 it had had only 26 churches and chapels and 27 priests. Growth was slow: by 1881 the number of churches, chapels and Mass stations had risen to 49, served by only 43 priests; by 1901, there were 63 places for public worship, and the number of priests had risen to 69. There were a few Catholic commentators in the 1890s who believed that the realities of this missionary situation had been ignored in the rush to expand in the urban centres by building large, permanent churches, and to keep resident priests in every rural parish – priests who were likely to be underemployed for much of their time. What was needed, wrote one of them, were communities of priests and the setting up of teams of missionary catechists. Pope Leo XIII accepted the logic of these arguments when he wrote to Cardinal Vaughan to say that he did not expect English Catholics to subscribe to Catholic causes elsewhere because they had 'millions of heathens and heretics to evangelize' at home; even the annual Peter's Pence collection might, he argued, be reduced or used for these missionary purposes.[3]

What was the position in London? It seems that at the turn of the century there were about 200,000 Catholics in inner London. The religious census of 1902 showed that about 37 per cent of them attended Mass regularly, though other estimates give an average of no more than 30 per cent as the attendance rate. There is good evidence that even where practice was relatively low the percentage of children who were sent to the Catholic schools was high – 80 per cent in Walworth, and a massive 95 per cent in Rotherhithe. A priest in Fulham reckoned that the 'rough poor', like the costers, hardly ever went to church but still sent their children to the local parish school. Statistics for the diocese of Westminster are.[4]

	1890	1900	1910	% increase
Secular clergy	253	288	371	47.0
Regular clergy	100	127	170	70.0
Public churches and chapels	124	153	176	42.0
Average school attendance	21,013	26,528	31,342	49.0

Clearly, there was much to be satisfied with, and Catholicism was enjoying rates of growth not matched by other denominations; it was not a time for standing still or being defensive. While the increases were satisfying, the clergy knew of the work to be done both to prevent serious leakage from the faith among the young once they had left school, and to continue to expand into new areas to match the movements of population.

Writers at the time who described the Catholic Church in England liked to draw a picture of a church made up socially of two very unequal parts: a small but influential 'top' composed of aristocrats and landed gentry, the remnants of the old recusant Catholicism, and a very large 'bottom' of working class and poor members, mainly the result of the large Irish immigration in the middle of the century. This image was used at the time (and has been used by historians since) to show that Catholics still existed only at the margins of English society, and that their religion had failed to make any significant headway into that bastion of Victorian England – the middle classes. The picture could be supported statistically but had begun to change before the end of the Queen's reign and was, in any case, more complex than was often made out.

The aristocratic 'top' certainly existed. In 1900 there were 41 Catholic peers of Great Britain and Ireland, 54 baronets and 28 knights. Not all of these were of ancient Catholic families for some were converts and a few were recent creations. They were led at the very top by the fifteenth Duke of Norfolk, Earl Marshal of England, who had succeeded to the title in 1860, come of age in 1868, and was to live until 1917. He has been described as the last duke to possess that legendary quality which sentiment used to attribute to noble lords before they were replaced by the royal family in popular interest and esteem. Whatever his personal contribution to the Catholic cause was, and it seems to have been considerable, as a body the Catholic peers have been accurately depicted as very respectable in character, solid in quality, seldom erratic, rarely brilliant and politically distinctly inactive.[5] English Catholics, however, were proud of them and of their undoubted Englishness, as well as of the pomp and circumstance which they brought to Catholic public occasions. More prosaically, their wealth was also important and a number of them contributed in an extremely generous way to the building of churches and schools – and cathedrals.

The landed gentry were still part of the Catholic body, too. Their numbers had been increased by the addition of a number of converts in the mid-Victorian period, who brought with them into the Catholic fold some of the oldest names in the country like Scrope, Ferrers and de Lisle, to stand alongside the Welds, the Blundells, the Cliffords and the Vaughans. As David Mathew put it, the new names seemed almost too good to be true to a generation which valued that form of truth.[6] It is, perhaps, too easy to romanticize these families and the life they led. On the whole they played little part in politics or local administration. They still held fast to the recusant tradition of quiet survival and superior religious beliefs, which had kept them going for so long that they made little use of their new freedoms. It is, perhaps, also too easy to single out the exceptional family such as the Vaughans, and to speak of its virtues, its certainties, and its solid, deep and unshowy devotion as typical of these old families. And if Cardinal Vaughan can be said to have summed up in himself the strengths of centuries of persecution, it should not be forgotten that that inheritance had its weaknesses as well.

The group that is normally omitted from the picture of late Victorian Catholicism is that of the middle-class Catholics. The steady rise of this group in the half century after the Restoration of the Hierarchy still awaits its historian who will chart the increasing number of doctors, lawyers (with a few going on to the bench), bankers, civil servants, military men and industrialists who can be found subscribing to Catholic charities and adding another layer of respectability to English Catholicism. Their existence is obvious from even a cursory examination of the *Catholic Directories* of those years, for these are full of advertisements for Catholic independent secondary schools (both day and boarding) which must have catered very largely for the children of Catholic middle-class families (and, it must be admitted, their non-Catholic neighbours in many cases). What is particularly striking is the number of schools which existed for the daughters of these families. In 1850 there were 19 fee-paying secondary schools for girls run by religious orders; this had risen to 83 in 1880, to 128 in 1900 and to 178 in 1910. All of these schools had a strong boarding element. Indeed in most cases this predominated. It is interesting that the first reference to any of these establishments' preparing girls for the Oxford and Cambridge examinations appeared in 1880, when eight schools did so. Within ten years 25 were doing so, and by the turn of the century 79 of the 128; by 1910 it is rare to find a school not doing so.[7] If further evidence is needed of the existence of a Catholic middle class it can be found in the fact that early in the new century there were enough names to fill a sizeable volume of a new annual publication, *The Catholic Who's Who* – a sure sign of having 'arrived' in middle-class circles.

There were converts to swell the numbers here, as well, and they and their families produced a number of leading priests, particularly for the religious orders – for example, Fr Henry Coleridge sj, the brother of the Lord Chief Justice, and the well-known Redemptorist, Fr Bridgett, son of a Derby silk manufacturer.[8] There were three convert bishops in addition to Manning. Most of the converts, of course, remained lay people. They did not stand out as a separate group in the same way as the early Oxford converts had done; what they wanted was to merge with Catholic neighbours and friends and become part of the Catholic body. But they did bring with them different traditions, and these helped to develop and change the outlook and concerns of their new co-religionists. They were more used to getting involved in local politics and the range of social interests so favoured by the late Victorian middle classses. The charities they supported were not restricted to Catholic concerns, and they accepted easily the responsibility of the leadership that was expected of them. Many of them saw no reason to abandon such involvement just because they had changed their religion, and they argued that the lay person's vocation should include a similar involvement and commitment. They felt that this was particularly important for Catholic women; as one of them wrote, well-to-do Catholic girls seemed to think of life in terms either of a vocation to a religious order or of extreme frivolity – they saw no middle way.[9] A look at the key roles played by some of these converts in movements such as the Catholic Women's League, the Catholic Social Guild and the Catholic Suffrage Society shows how important their contributions were. Bishop Casartelli of Salford (1903–25) claimed that the coming century would be the 'age of the laity'.[10] If that age was to be a fruitful one for the Church then the question of lay leadership had to be addressed; the dominance of the Catholic gentry had long gone, and the lay converts did something to show how the gap which their going had left might be filled. An involvement in public life at the local level was also important in the creation of a more acceptable image of Catholicism as a help towards a fuller integration into English society. That society had admired Catholic charitable work for a long time; the need now was for Catholics to turn outwards from their own concerns to those of society at large.

In this context, Cardinal Manning lamented that so few English Catholics entered the House of Commons; he took it as a sign of the hostility and social ostracism that they had to face once they tried to mount the national stage, but it is not clear how far this was the cause or how far the failure was due to a lack of Catholics wanting to do so. In 1894 there were just five Catholic Members representing English constituencies, and one of those was the very Irish T. P. O'Connor, one of the Members for Liverpool. There was another block of Catholic Members which was very much larger, made up as it was of about eighty Irish Members. On occasion they could hold the balance of power in the House and they were a key element in the strength of the Liberal Party. Their value to the English Catholic community is much more difficult to assess. They were not a popular parliamentary group as their one interest appeared to be Ireland and the Home Rule issue, which was hardly surprising. They were accused of not playing a full role in the life of the House and of reducing every other issue to a question of its value as a bargaining counter in the Home Rule struggle. In the public mind they were, quite unfairly, linked to the violence which more extreme groups were occasionally resorting to in both Ireland and England, and there was, anyway, a considerable residue of anti-Irish feeling in the country. To that extent they probably added to the prejudices of those who regarded Catholicism as un-English, and so hindered integration. On the other hand they were often in the limelight, and they played an important part in the fight for due recognition and support to be given to Catholic schools. As the justice of the call for Home Rule became more widely accepted and the House of Commons endorsed it by passing a number of bills in its favour, the Irish Catholic Members also became more readily assimilated under John Redmond's quiet leadership. This was part of a slow movement towards greater integration which was helped forward by the success of a small number of Catholics who did achieve high office, and by the more relaxed attitude of the new king, Edward VII. He was the first English monarch to visit the Pope since the Reformation, and he agreed with those who sought to change or get rid of the 'Coronation Oath', or Declaration before Parliament, with its insulting references to his Catholic subjects.[11]

Cardinal Manning had been involved in high matters of state and was respected even by those who were generally suspicious of his co-religionists. Completly English by upbringing, he had identified himself most closely not with the old Catholic landed families, nor with the well-to-do converts like himself, but with the Irish. A great amount has been written about the impact of the massive Irish immigration of the mid-century on the English Catholic Church, and of the problems it caused. There were not enough churches or priests to serve the newcomers, and thousands were lost before provision could be made for them. They were poor and forced to live in squalid conditions in the most crowded parts of the towns and cities. Many English people, including some English Catholics, found their presence disturbing and, as a defence, exaggerated their cultural differences and dwelt on their faults and foibles. Since about 80 per cent of the Irish were Catholic they suffered from the hostility to Catholicism that permeated English society at the time and which could break out into violence all too easily. Historians have argued whether the Irish were discriminated against because they were Catholics, or Catholics were discriminated against because of their association with the Irish; it made little difference, anyway, to those suffering from the discrimination.[12]

While the initial immigration caused problems for the English Catholic church as it had been slowly re-emerging in the 1840s and 1850s, it also created opportunites which for the most part were well used. Rapid expansion resulted in the building of a very strong urban base at a time when English society was becoming predominantly urban. Schools had to be built and new styles of service and devotion introduced. Some might turn up their noses at these popular, 'Roman' practices, but they were essential if large working-class congregations were to be attracted and held. One gets the impression that some of those who were liturgically fastidious about these things were at heart more disgusted by the masses than by their supposedly emotional devotions. The dedication of the clergy to the task of providing for their people, and their success in moulding the disparate elements of English Catholicism into a whole, deserve greater recognition. Their contemporaries gave due praise for the way social problems were tackled, schools built and charitable work undertaken; the self-sacrifice of the slum priest and the religious sister became a commonplace in the writings of social commentators, and was often held up as an example to other denominations.

By 1900 much had changed. The Irish had benefited from the slow increase in prosperity and the expansion of opportunity which the working classes as a whole had enjoyed. Second and third generation members of the Irish community had moved successfully into commerce, journalism, the law and the medical profession; more recent immigrants had come with better qualifications and had gone directly into the civil service, banking and teaching. If it was not a tale of 'from rags to riches' for more than a handful, at least it was one of from rags to respectability for many. Of course many were still poor and, like their English counterparts, wholly taken up with the daily struggle to survive economically and provide for their families; as the new century began they faced a worsening economic situation and increased insecurity. Priests in London in charge of largely Irish working-class parishes spoke of the basic loyalty of their people, their attachment to the priest and the faith even if they rarely went to church; regular practice rates of 20 to 25 per cent were not unusual, and in some poor parishes the rate was nearer to 12 per cent. Non-Catholic observers commented favourably that the Catholic poor were different from their fellows; as Charles Booth put it, 'they are a class apart, being as a rule devout and willing to contribute something towards the support of their schools and the maintenance of their religion'. It is too easy, perhaps, to romanticize the relationship between the casual Catholic and his or her religion. Much of the praise seems to stem from a comparison between them and their fully secularized non-Catholic neighbours. Some priests were very critical of the indifference shown by many of their people, and knew only too well how the young very often did not share even the residual Catholicism of their parents.[13]

While Irish Catholics and their descendants numerically made up the greatest part of the Church in England, they did not capture and dominate it in the same way as their compatriots did the Catholic Church in Australia and the United States of America. Only three of the bishops who ruled English dioceses from 1850 to 1910 were Irish by birth – at times a cause of resentment among the Irish Catholic community. Manning, for all his Irish sympathies, probably had too strong an influence on episcopal appointments and wished to avoid any embarrassment with the English government over the elevation of priests with overtly Irish political sympathies. He also wanted to increase the proportion of English bishops who had been trained in Rome. No doubt the powerful lobby of the aristocratic and 'old' Catholic families played a part, too, in keeping 'their' Church as English as possible. For, however well the Irish became assimilated to English society, they remained Irish in outlook and sympathies. When they were interested in politics it was in Irish politics and the Home Rule issue; most were slow to get involved in English affairs, and they were often the despair of English working-class leaders because of their lack of interest in either trade unions or the emerging Labour Party. Manning had understood their outlook and openly supported the cause of 'justice for Ireland', though even he fell far short of the full nationalist ideal. Cardinal Vaughan did not understand it at all, and had no sympathy with those who espoused it; as his biographer said, Ireland was a question which was 'outside his life'. Quite apart from any question of principle (such as keeping the Empire intact) he did not want to lose the Irish MPs from Westminster because they were useful in the schools debate and on other Catholic issues. He was also aware of the danger of a bishop taking sides in political matters and so of presenting the Church to the English people in a prejudicial light. His failure to adopt Irish aspirations as his own, or at least to sympathize with them, made him unpopular with many of his people.[14]

There was one matter which *did* bind the English Catholic Church together, and that was education. There was a complex interweaving of issues here, the least important of which was an interest in education for its own sake. It would not have been possible to get Catholics of all classes to attend rallies in their thousands, and to contribute huge sums of money, if the cause had been just that of intellectual improvement. There was a genuine fear of losing Catholic young people to Protestantism or secularism if they did not have their own schools to attend. The board schools, established as a result of the 1870 Education Act, were regarded as particularly dangerous; indeed, neutral observers wondered at the hatred directed at them by the Catholic clergy.[15] The schools question produced a strong sense of sacrifice on the one hand and of persecution on the other, and both of these are standard ingredients in the cohesion of minority groups. Both, too, had been key components in the background experiences of English and Irish Catholics, and so struck a chord in their psychological make-up. Huge demonstrations could be organized and otherwise apathetic Catholics galvanized into action by the mere hint of 'a threat to our schools'; there seemed to be many such threats about in the years of educational reform after 1870, and in 1902 and 1906 when the Liberals launched their attacks on the voluntary schools. Bishops and priests came to rely on the group loyalty that resulted, and this reliance became another factor which helped to keep the issue live. The strain on resources was considerable, but few, if any, questioned the necessity to find the money somehow. The provision of schools did not, of course, stop the leakage of the young from the faith but it kept many in touch who might otherwise have lost contact altogether.

There were some who took a broader view than this and realized the importance of providing education for other reasons, too. Bishop Casartelli wrote that it was not just a question of the Catholics' right to have their children educated in the safety of a Catholic atmosphere. He argued that there was a need for good Catholic secondary schools to enable Catholics to be educated into being good citizens, for they had to learn to accept the duties of citizenship as well as enjoying its fruits and should not be content with merely Catholic activities. Without good schools, he went on, Catholics would become the permanent underclass of the social system, and would never be able to take their proper part in public life.[16] Secondary education was clearly of growing importance to the Catholic body as their middle-class representation increased. The question of a university education was of interest to only a few, as was true of the general population, but to those few it was very important. Manning's attempt to set up a Catholic university met the fate expected by most observers, but he continued to uphold fanatically the ban on attendance at Oxford and Cambridge. In this he was supported by the other bishops, including Vaughan when he was Bishop of Salford. He was happy to defer to Manning's personal experience of university life (which Vaughan had never had) and fears of the effect that Oxbridge would have on the faith of Catholic undergraduates. Here again was the fear of leakage – and a sad mistrust of the strength of the faith of the young after years of intenseively Catholic secondary education. By the 1890s, the numbers ignoring the ban, or getting around it by dispensation, were on the rise. As other forms of university education became increasingly available the ban on the old universities became harder to justify. Eventually Vaughan listened to those who argued for a change (mainly lay people but also some clergy) and took the lead in getting Propaganda in Rome to agree to its being lifted altogether. While the affair was not of practical interest to very many Catholics, it had a symbolic importance in removing another cause of isolation: for too long Catholics at that level had been educated apart and in a different, largely foreign, tradition. Unfortunately this was to remain the case for a long time in the main Catholic institutions of higher education in England, the seminaries.[17]

Not that Catholic England lacked people of letters or journals and reviews of standing: *The Tablet*, the *Downside Review*, *The Month*, the *Dublin Review* were of high quality, particularly strong on literature, Continental news and scholarship. As a historian has said of them, they were marked by a humane breadth and depth derived partly from cherishing their recusant past and partly from their consciousness of a European inheritance.[18] There was the outstanding scholar, Lord Acton, who became Regius Professor of Modern History at Cambridge and founded the massive *Cambridge Modern History*. He was, perhaps, more Continental than English ('I never had any contemporaries', he said on one occasion). More homebred were historians like Edmund Bishop (outstanding for his liturgical studies), Cardinal Gasquet and Herbert Thurston, and the historian-cum-biographer Wilfrid Ward, whose combined output was evidence of serious scholarship of a high calibre. There were almost enough poets to fill an anthology – Coventry Patmore, the Meynells, Francis Thompson, Lionel Johnson, Ernest Dowson and the young Belloc among them – and, of course, Gerard Manley Hopkins whose work was still unknown at this time. There were novelists galore, many of whom were household names in their day; in some of their works, one writer has claimed, sentimentality reached the point of saturation.[19] They are now forgotten, but at the time they witnessed to the richness of the world of Catholic letters, enlarged as it had been by the accession of the converts. Of theology and scriptural studies there was far less that was noteworthy; the seminaries were dedicated to turning out priests with a high sense of their pastoral mission, and in this they were very successful. What genuine intellectual enquiry there was in these fields was soon to be snuffed out by the dead hand of the Modernist crisis.

Catholics were becoming more acceptable in the wider community, but there was still hostility – even though Manning could speak of its having become a 'more civilised hostility'. Catholic separateness was disliked and regulations regarding mixed marriages, for example, were deeply resented because of the promises which had to be made about the upbringing of the children as Catholics. Perhaps the urban Catholic parish had become too successful in its attempts to be all things to all parishioners. It wanted to keep the members of its flock untainted by the secular world in which they lived and worked, and so provided social clubs, religious confraternities and sodalities, savings and loan clubs, schools, home visits by the priest and by lay collectors. Ordinary Catholics were thus tied to their church in a way not found among their Protestant fellow workers, even if they were church or chapel goers.[20] Perhaps, also, there was too much talk of the conversion of England, often in an aggressive tone, for relations between Catholics and other Christians to be other than prickly at best. The tiny movement in the 1890s to bring about some form of corporate reunion between Anglicanism and Rome was genuinely incomprehensible to most English Catholics (and to most Anglicans, too, for that matter). Vaughan found it amusing until it took up too much of his time and he saw it as a hindrance to individual conversions. Then it became a nuisance to be got rid of as quickly as possible. The condemnation of Anglican Orders as worthless by the Pope in 1896 was welcomed by most as a statement of the obvious, despite the reservations of a few (including the Duke of Norfolk and Bishop Brownlow of Clifton) about the triumphalist stance taken by the victors in the controversy.[21]

So this was Cardinal Vaughan's flock. He was not a charismatic figure, nor even always a popular one. While his apprentice years had not given him immediate pastoral experience, they had proved his administrative ability, his sense of priorities and his deep and uncomplicated personal devotion. If this makes him sound worthy but pedestrian the image is incomplete, for these traits and skills were put to work to realize a number of ideals which were his genuine motivations – whether it was the founding of a successful missionary congregation or the building of a great cathedral which should become the apostolic centre of the nation.

NOTES

Archive sources.· Most of the archive material for this book is to be found in the Archives of the Archbishop of Westminster, referred to in the notes as AAW. The cataloguing system in the Archives is mainly a chronological one, based on the period of office of each Archbishop. Each Archbishop is referred to by an initial letter or letters, for example V for Cardinal Vaughan, Hi for Cardinal Hinsley, Go for Cardinal Godfrey. Other material is to be found in separately named boxes. Plans are currently in hand to move the principal Cathedral materials from the Archives to Cathedral House, so that there will be a separate Cathedral Archive.

1   The standard life of Cardinal Vaughan is J. G. Snead-Cox, *The Life of Cardinal Vaughan* (2 vols, 1912).
2   For statistics, see G. A. Beck (ed.), *The English Catholics 1850–1950* (1950); R. Currie, A. Gilbert and L. Horsley, *Churches and Churchgoers* (Oxford, 1977); O. Chadwick, *The Victorian Church* (2 vols; 2nd edn, 1972). Quotation from L. Hollen Lees, *Exiles of Erin* (Manchester, 1979), pp. 175–6.
3   See Beck; *Catholic Directories* for relevant years; J. D. Holmes, *More Roman Than Rome* (1978), pp. 249ff.
4   See H. M. McLeod, *Class and Religion in the Late Victorian City* (1974), and *Catholic Directories*.
5   D. Mathew, *Catholicism in England* (1936), pp. 218, 233.
6   Ibid., p. 219.
7   I am indebted to Wendy Higgins for these statistics based on her examination of the *Catholic Directories*.
8   See Mathew, p. 216 for a full list.
9   V. Crawford, *Ideals of Charity* (1908).
10 L. C. Casartelli, preface to C. Plater, *Retreats for the People* (1912).
11 E. Oldmeadow, *Francis Cardinal Bourne* (2 vols, 1940, 1944), II, pp. 46–55; it was finally altered in 1910.
12 On the Irish in Britain see Beck; McLeod; Lees; and R. Swift and S. Gilley, *The Irish in the Victorian City* (1985).
13 McLeod, pp. 41, 75–6.
14 Snead-Cox, I, pp. 470–3; E. R. Norman, *The English Catholic Church in the 19th Century* (1989), p. 355.
15 McLeod, p. 99.
16 L. C. Casartelli, *Signs of the Times* (Salford, 1903), pp. 9–11; and *The Federationist* (Salford, January 1910).
17 On the universities question see Holmes and Beck.
18 Chadwick, II, p. 409.
19 Beck, ch. XVII; Holmes, pp. 234ff.; Mathew, p. 237.
20 Chadwick, II, p. 407; McLeod, pp. 77–8.
21 Holmes, pp. 218–24; Snead-Cox, II, *passim*.

Chapter 2

Cardinal Vaughan:
an idealist in a hurry

'COULD I LEAVE 20,000 children without education, and drain my friends and my flock to pile up stones and bricks?' So spoke Cardinal Manning at a meeting which had been called to organize the collection of money for the building of a cathedral as a memorial to his predecessor, Cardinal Wiseman. It was a striking statement and has been often quoted; it fits in with the image which we have of the 'Cardinal of the poor', with his genuine concern for the condition of his people, and especially of the poor Irish among them. He saw the provision of education as of prime importance, both to keep them from lapsing from the faith and to enable them to improve their position in society. In the circumstances, to put much effort or money into building a cathedral would be aiming for 'cloud-cuckoo land'.[1] The quotation has also been used to point up a supposed difference between Manning and Vaughan: the practical, socially aware pastor on the one hand, and the triumphalist, and remote, idealist on the other. It is, then, surprising to learn that Manning accepted the need for a cathedral in London from the very beginning, and that this was not just an early enthusiasm which became dimmed when he discovered the extent of the problems facing him as Archbishop. He continued to be interested and involved in the matter throughout his time at Westminster, and few things would have given him more satisfaction in his last ten years than to have been able to build a fitting cathedral.

As early as 1865 Manning said that the project was in accordance with his wishes and that he would gladly take up 'the burden of labouring for the rest of his life' to carry it through. Westminster, he felt, needed a cathedral 'proportionate to the chief diocese of the Catholic Church in England, and to the chief city of the British Empire'. The need to provide education for the poor would have to take precedence, but work on the cathedral project carried on. First of all a site was bought in Carlisle Place in 1867 for £16,500, and the architect Henry Clutton began to design a building to fit the very awkwardly shaped plot, which measured 488 feet by 85. Before he had finished, the Cardinal bought an adjoining plot for a further £20,000 and so Clutton returned to the drawing board. Then a building known as the Guards' Institute was bought by Manning in 1872 with his own money as a replacement Archbishop's House; this helped to enlarge the area of the original plots, and Clutton changed his plans again and came up with a plan for a gigantic Gothic structure which would have been 450 feet long and 250 feet wide. There certainly was not enough money to think about starting on such a building; Manning approved Clutton's plans, knowing that that was the end of them.[2]

The Cardinal had not, however, given up the idea of having a cathedral. Within a few years he was beginning to think that the work for the poor children could be said to be done, and when, in 1882, it looked as though a wealthy patron might be willing to cover all the costs, his enthusiasm was rekindled. He launched an appeal to free the site of its remaining debt, and this was quickly successful: eight contributors, who were later given the title of 'Cathedral Pioneers', contributed over £29,000 – among them were the Cardinal himself, the Duke of Norfolk, Baron Petre, Baron Gerrard and Baroness Weld. The cathedral was to be in the style of the Votive Church in Vienna, and was designed by a well-known Austrian architect, von Ferstel. The Cardinal decided that an even better site could be obtained, and so negotiated to buy the site of the old Middlesex County Prison in Tothill Fields, Westminster, which was up for sale at £115,000. A complicated series of manoeuvres through a specially set up land company resulted in the end in the Cardinal having half the new site for the proposed cathedral and a mortgage of £20,000; the original sites and the rest of the new one were sold off. It is not altogether clear what went wrong. Cardinal Vaughan's biographer says that Manning was 'slowly undeceived' about the intentions or the ability of the benefactor, a Sir Tatton Sykes; another story is that the latter laid down such conditions as could not be met. There is, to the modern reader, something odd about the story of the Viennese architect and his completed plans, and about the non-Catholic donor, although *The Tablet* took it all seriously enough and even published an illustration of the Votive

The caption reads: "The map shows the complete Tothill Fields Prison site which Cardinal Manning bought through the Westminster Land Company. The dividing line through the prison building marks the line of the present Ambrosden Avenue. To the left of Morpeth Terrace are the two earlier sites bought by the Cardinal; note their irregular shapes. The plot marked 'Archbishop's House' was the former Guards' Institute, also bought by the Cardinal. (The map appeared in The Tablet (10 May 1884).)"

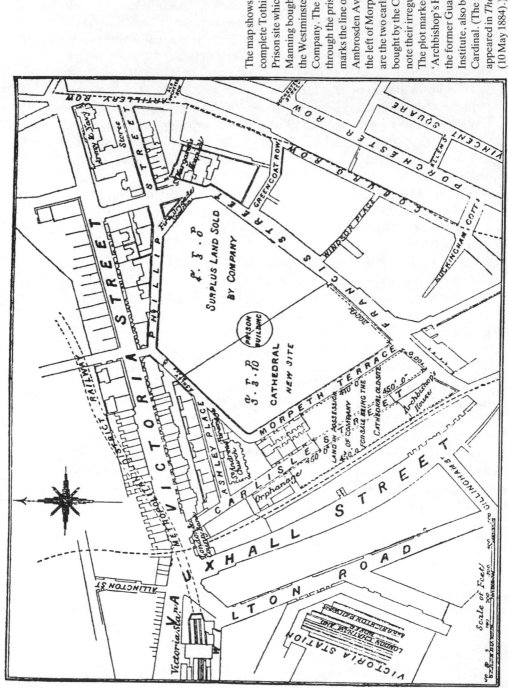

The map shows the complete Tothill Fields Prison site which Cardinal Manning bought through the Westminster Land Company. The dividing line through the prison building marks the line of the present Ambrosden Avenue. To the left of Morpeth Terrace are the two earlier sites bought by the Cardinal; note their irregular shapes. The plot marked 'Archbishop's House' was the former Guards' Institute, also bought by the Cardinal. (The map appeared in *The Tablet* (10 May 1884).)

Church in Vienna. Whatever the reasons, Manning was very disappointed. But at least a site now existed that would accommodate a good sized building, and a small fund had been established towards the costs of building it by the extra generosity of some of the 'Pioneers'.[3]

The choice of Herbert Vaughan, then Bishop of Salford, to succeed Manning as Archbishop in 1892 seems to have surprised no one. His decision to involve himself immediately in the cathedral project did, however, cause some misgivings. There were, of course, those who doubted the ability of the English Catholic body to raise enough money, and feared that a half-finished building would remain as a lasting reproach to the pretentiousness of Catholic attempts to imitate their Church of England neighbours. It was also the age of the 'social gospel', and there were objections from those who believed that if such large sums of money could be raised they would be better spent on the poor and other good causes. To suggest that Vaughan was insensitive to such needs and went ahead with building a cathedral because he was a triumphalist bricks and mortar prelate is to misunderstand him altogether. His work for the poor in Salford, his setting up of the Crusade of Rescue there, and later in London, to help Catholic children, his deep concern about the problem of leakage from the faith, his later establishment of the Catholic Social Union, and, of course, the founding of the great Mill Hill missionary movement – these were the actions of a caring pastor. It is true that his reserved manner often gave the impression that he was more interested in administration and money-raising than in dealing directly with people, but the skills he had in both those areas were, to use a modern phrase, people-centred – and God-centred. For Vaughan was critical of the social gospel in one respect. As his biographer put it, he believed that one of the strongest tendencies of the time was to 'treat the Service of Man as though it were an all-sufficient substitute for the Service of God', and so to identify religion entirely with the corporal works of mercy. To support the building of a cathedral would be, in the circumstances, 'a public profession of faith on the part of his people'; a sign of their belief in the 'reality and value of a purely spiritual good'.[4]

At the same time, he thought that a cathedral would be good for the national image of English Catholics. He believed that they had made such progress in the previous fifty years that a cathedral in the capital had become almost a necessity if that progress were to continue and increase. It would signal to others their revival and confidence, and as the Duke of Norfolk was to say at the laying of the foundation stone (quoting Newman), 'If the Catholic people were to build up the Church again in England, the great work was not to be done in a corner'.[5] It is interesting that Vaughan hoped that the cathedral would be ready in time to host the celebrations for the golden jubilee of the Restoration of the Hierarchy in 1900, for he believed that only part of the task of restoring English Catholicism to the full life of the Church had been undertaken in 1850. The setting up of the bishops and the regularization of the life of the Church had been an important public symbol that the 'sort of stunted and maimed life' which had been the result of the years of persecution was passing, but there had remained a crucial area in which English Catholicism was still lacking. That area, for Vaughan, was the daily and public worship of the Church.

At the laying of the foundation stone Vaughan stated very clearly what the future cathedral would provide: it would be a place where the sacred liturgy of the Church should be carried out in all its fullness day by day, and many times a day, as it was of old in Westminster and in Canterbury. This public prayer, he continued, was something that had been lost, and without it the Catholic Church in England was deprived and disadvantaged – even if most Catholics were unaware of their loss. This vision of a house of prayer functioning in the centre of London on behalf of others and winning them graces was a fundamental element in Vaughan's thinking at this time. Whatever else might be subject to compromise in his plans for the cathedral, this had to remain untouched: the full, daily Divine Office would be carried out there with as much dignity and ceremonial as possible. He accepted the old adage that churches are buildings with which, as well as in which, we worship God, and he used it to justify the building of the cathedral itself. But he was always clear that it would be what went on in it that would be its ultimate justification.[6]

Having decided that the Divine Office should be recited and sung daily in the cathedral, Vaughan had to find a body of priests who would be responsible for doing this. From the beginning he seems to have been clear in his own mind that the most obvious people to ask to do this would be the English Benedictine monks: the daily singing of the Office was an integral part of their vocation, and they carried it out with reverence and beauty. Moreover, it would be very fitting from a historical perspecive to bring the Benedictines back to Westminster, for they had served the Abbey in the centuries before the Reformation. As his biographer says, this seemed to him to be such a sensible and obvious solution to the problem that he just took it for granted, and on a number of occasions he announced publicly that it would happen. He was so certain about it, indeed, that he ordered the architect to include in the plans a specially large area (or 'retro-choir') behind the altar to accommodate a large body of monks.[7]

For a man so skilled in administration, and well used to the intricacies of negotiation, it is strange that he had consulted neither the Benedictines nor the Westminster secular clergy before making some of these pronouncements. His first plan was that the Benedictines from Downside should open a new monastery at Ealing in London, and from there serve both the pastoral needs of the local Catholics and the liturgical needs of the new cathedral; they would also say Mass, preach and hear confessions. The parish attached to the cathedral, however, should be served by diocesan secular priests, so that there would be two sets of clergy using the building and carrying out pastoral duties there. Possibilities of friction and resentment seemed to be almost built into these proposals. The Benedictines accepted the proposals initially and a small number of monks moved to Ealing in 1897. It should be pointed out that the English Benedictines were very unusual in that they took a so-called 'missionary oath' which bound them to work in a pastoral capacity in the 'missions' or parishes of the country; most of their members did not live a monastic life in the ordinary sense of the word.[8]

The Cardinal began to have doubts about his proposals, perhaps because of the concern which members of his Chapter were expressing about possible clashes of interest. He thought that the problem lay in the 'missionary oath' taken by the English Benedictines; this made it very difficult to tie them to a purely liturgical role in the cathedral. To avoid this he made an amazing next move: he approached the French Benedictines at the famous abbey at Solesmes (who were truly monastic and, moreover, renowned for their plainsong) and offered the position at Westminster to them – and this without consulting the English Benedictines at all! The French responded positively, though they admitted that they could only supply a very small number of monks; perhaps their English brethren could send some as well? What they wanted, after a trial period, was to build a fully French house at Westminster. These negotiations went on for almost a year, and then Vaughan approached the English monks again to see if they would agree to the French taking on the work at the cathedral. It should have come as no surprise to him that, far from agreeing, they were deeply insulted both by the suggestion itself and by his failure to deal openly with themselves. The whole episode certainly shows the Cardinal in a bad light. It was extremely insensitive of him to suggest that the English Benedictines might be willing to give up to the French their centuries-long connection with Westminster just when there appeared to be a chance to re-establish it. Not to inform the English superiors that he was approaching another, and foreign, group of monks was plainly discourteous, and it was not possible to re-establish good relations with them in the immediate aftermath. He abandoned his plan to have the Benedictines at Westminster.

He turned instead to the secular clergy of the diocese and announced his change of plans at the diocesan Synod in 1901. He told his priests that they would have to provide a high standard of church music and religious ceremonial. Plans for how the clergy would be organized, he went on, were before the Chapter. The Catholic press reported that the secular clergy were 'overjoyed and eager'; while there had been sentimental reasons for wanting the monks back at Westminster, it was much more fitting that a Cathedral which was meant to serve the whole of the Catholic body should not be the preserve of one particular order. Finally, it was reported that the Cardinal had already obtained permission from Rome to increase the number of canons from twelve to eighteen, and to establish a body of secular clergy to act as Cathedral Chaplains.[9]

While the performance of the official liturgy in the new Cathedral was Vaughan's chief concern, linked as it was with his belief in the centrality of worship and prayer in the life of any church, he also had a broader vision. He frequently spoke of his desire for a 'live Cathedral' which would be 'the head and heart of the life of the Church in England.' It was to house a body of priests whose lives should be examples to the rest of the diocese. In another of his phrases, he described it as a 'Catholic arsenal' from which lecturers and missionaries would go out suitably armed, and which would be the meeting place and inspiration for lay groups of all kinds. Its library would be used by theological students throughout the land, and its ceremonial would provide a model for all to follow. He appealed to people's patriotism when asking them for money: London was the capital of the British Empire and the highest city of the world, and so its Cathedral must embody the greatness of the capital and of Great Britain. He believed that 'every member of every flock in the country' was interested in 'this House of the Lord' being set up near 'the ancient shrine of the old religion of the land'.[10]

To try to achieve all of this, once the rows with the Benedictines were over, the Cardinal laid down in considerable detail the arrangements for its liturgy, its administration and its clergy. What he would have liked would have been a chapter of residential canons living around the Cathedral to sing and recite the Divine Office each day and to form a community which would have made the Cathedral an apostolic centre for the diocese. In the formal 'Constitution for the government of the Metropolitan Cathedral', which he issued in 1902, he hoped that 'before very long' the daily liturgy would be

John Francis Bentley, 1839–1902:
Architect of the Cathedral

Cardinal Herbert Vaughan, Archbishop
of Westminster 1892–1903, founder of the
Cathedral

Laying the foundation stone, 29 June 1895. Bentley
is kneeling centre rear, facing the camera

Early interior; notice the plain piers. The Stations
are in but the present balustrades are not there

Early interior; interlocking arches and beautiful carved capitals, each designed individually by Bentley. Photo: Newbery Smith

carried out by the full Chapter of Canons, assisted by others, and that the Chapter could then take its proper share of the administration of the Cathedral. In practice, however, the tradition of having this type of Chapter had not been restored alongside the bishops in 1850, and most of the canons in an English Catholic diocese were busy parish priests who met together usually only once a month for their capitular High Mass and formal business meeting. To take their place in the Cathedral he set up a College of Chaplains, composed of secular priests who would be residential; there were a small number of non-residential ones given the title of Prebendaries; the two were indistinguishable in practice. The College was to number between eighteen and twenty-four Chaplains who would have their own Rector, who would regulate their duties and ensure that at least three-quarters of the College were in attendance for the Cathedral services at any one time. Any Chaplain who arrived late, or who was absent without due cause, would be fined 'according to the practice in the Roman basilicas'. Each Chaplain was entitled to one week free from choral duties in every month, and to one free month every year for vacation – this arrangement was later changed to the Chaplains' having alternate weeks on and off choral duty. Finally, all were to wear a distinctive choir dress, which could not be used outside the Cathedral unless the Chaplains were attending the Archbishop as a College.

Vaughan was not content with this rather legalistic approach. In a second official document later in the same year, he set out the principles which he hoped would inspire the Chaplains and convince them of the value of their office.[11] As he said in the Introduction, no body of people, no matter how competent and devoted they might be, could maintain 'unity of purpose and action' unless that purpose and action be clearly defined and accepted by all its members. He believed that the needs of the Cathedral in this regard mirrored the needs of the country as a whole: both required a priesthood which was animated by the apostolic spirit, and this meant having men who dedicated themselves to a life of prayer and to the ministry of the Word. Whatever the need and taste for the activities which absorbed so large a portion of a priest's life, he had to be, in the first place, a man of prayer. There was nothing new in this ideal of course – it was the stock in trade of every clerical retreat-giver. Where Vaughan departed from the usual message was in insisting that the duty of prayer could be discharged by priests' devoting themselves to the public liturgical prayer of the Church – indeed, he argued that this was 'the highest function of the apostolic calling'. To support his case he pointed to the long tradition in the Church of having the Divine Office performed daily in cathedrals. Even though that tradition had been lost in many places, so that 'a mournful silence reigns in place of the daily chant of the Office', this should not happen in England, where the 'Church of St Augustine, St Anselm, St Thomas of Canterbury is slowly reviving'. The Cathedral was never intended to be a 'lifeless shell', he went on, but a 'body animated by its proper living soul', and that soul was the divine liturgy, accurately and fully rendered by the clergy and the choir, and 'pulsating from its heart throughout the entire body of the Church'. No mere human reasoning should persuade priests that 'this earnest, fervent work of praise and prayer' was not of the essence of the apostolic life.

Vaughan must have realized that he had a difficult case to win. As he himself admitted in the same document, so completely had the idea of the public recitation of the Divine Office, as the normal form of public worship of the Church, faded from people's minds in England, that even Catholics had come to regard it as 'a curious survival, and the peculiar heritage of ancient orders of monks and nuns'. And his appeal to pre-Reformation practice rang a little false: cathedrals in medieval England had been staffed not by ordinary members of the secular clergy but by either monks or religious orders of canons. If one adds to this the eminently successful development of an English missionary clergy throughout the nineteenth century, whose ideal was a commitment to an active parish apostolate and the extension of churches and schools, the Cardinal had little chance of success. Those priests recited their Breviaries faithfully every day but more, it seems, from a sense of duty than from a conviction that it was an essential part of their spiritual life; to ask them to see the public recitation of that Office as the peak of their apostolic ministry would require a mind-shift beyond the reach of all but a few. No one would have disagreed with Vaughan when he said that the Church in England needed holy and prayerful priests more than it needed priests devoted to preaching and zealous works; how far they would have agreed with his concluding appeal as anything more than a pious hope is open to question: 'The daily presence of the clergy in choir . . . gathered in spirit round the Queen of Apostles (to whom he had dedicated the College of Chaplains) . . . will secure the victory in many a battle with sin and error to be fought throughout this vast metropolis and throughout this Province of Westminster. Prayer wins more victories than this world wots of.' In this context the final archaism is rather telling.

In all that he wrote and spoke about the Cathedral Cardinal Vaughan made almost no mention of what is the basic function of a cathedral: it is the visible manifestation of the bishop's authority over his diocese, his 'seat' where the episcopal throne is and from which he exercises his twin roles of teaching and ruling. Vaughan's constant concern to portray it as a house of prayer, a source of grace and example, a miniature of the apostolic life to which the secular priest was called – all this was a counterbalance to any charge of ecclesiastical triumphalism. It was also in considerable contrast with the views of his successor, Cardinal Bourne. Many years later, on the occasion of the laying of the foundation stone of the new cathedral in Liverpool in 1933, Bourne was Papal Legate and spoke of the purpose of a cathedral in quite different terms. He argued that we could only understand the meaning of a cathedral in proportion to our understanding of the episcopal office. This office demanded that every bishop should have a centre of authority, a 'place both of honour and jurisdiction' to enable him to show forth the full splendour of Divine worship and to govern 'with due honour and effect' his flock, and 'whence may flow to his people all the gifts of which he has the keeping'. A cathedral, he went on, was meant to be the fullest external expression of 'this essential characteristic' of Christ's Church, to enshrine the throne of episcopal authority and to make clear the position which the Episcopate legitimately claimed.[12]

As well as arranging for the daily performance of the Divine Office in the Cathedral, Vaughan had to see to the practical running of the new Cathedral parish – as we have seen, this was one of the issues in the controversy about bringing in the Benedictines. From the outset Vaughan had intended that there should be such a parish – perhaps partly to ensure that there would be a natural congregation for the Cathedral – and his Constitution set out how that parish should be organized and administered. There is something strange about these initial arrangements, almost as though the parish was to be in the Cathedral but not of it. There was to be a 'Vicar of the Mission' in charge in place of the Archbishop, and he was to have assigned to him a number of assistant priests for the work of the parish. A chapel in the Cathedral was to be the parish church, but no services were to take place in it while Cathedral services were in progress. The times of the parish services had to be agreed with the priest in charge of the Cathedral services (known as the Prefect of the Sacristy). The Vicar of the Mission was to have a room on the ground floor of the tower as his parish office. The receipts from any collections taken in the Cathedral were to go to its Administrator, but 'stole fees' should go to the Vicar and his priests. The document is not altogether clear, but it seems that the assistant priests attached to the parish were to be separate from the College of Chaplains; in effect, the work of the parish would be running alongside that of the Cathedral, and the services in the latter would not be an integral part of the life of the parish.

These arrangements did not last long, and soon the Cathedral itself became the parish church and its Administrator the acting parish priest. The roles of the assistant priests were taken on by the Chaplains, and when the parish was divided into five districts, two or three of the Chaplains were appointed to take charge of each. It was presumably at this time that the Chaplains changed to a one-week-on and one-week-off rota, so that one of the two could always be free for parish duties.

The new system was better because it integrated the parish and the Cathedral, and avoided the 'church within a church' which could easily have arisen if the original plans had been carried through, with all the tensions that this would have caused. On the other hand, to give the Chaplains a dual role lessened the commitment to their choral duties and provided a rival attraction which, as things worked out, for many of them proved the stronger and thus created its own tensions. It was a tacit admission of defeat in terms of Vaughan's noble idea; it appears that his system was abandoned sometime after his death in 1903. The new system also gave the parish a unique parish church, which some worshippers found rather intimidating and in which it was difficult to build up a sense of belonging. It was also likely that there would be tensions, real or perceived, between the role and demands of that church as a diocesan, and even national, centre and its role of serving the local community.

The balance between these different demands would have to be kept by the Administrator. His duties were laid out in Vaughan's original Constitution: he was in charge of all the officials of the Cathedral; he must satisfy himself that they all carried out in a becoming manner their respective duties; he was to regulate and decide questions of contention between them, and to see that any directions of the Archbishop were duly followed. In addition, he was, originally, the Cathedral treasurer, but this was soon made into a separate office. The success with which Administrators carried out their role was going to be crucial in how the Cathedral would develop – in some ways even more crucial than the part to be played by successive Cardinals. Some would inevitably be better fitted for the role than others; some would have more of the diplomatic skills that the job required; some would be men of action and initiative; some would be content to keep matters going smoothly in a period of calm and consolidation; some would be faced with major crises – usually financial, occasionally arising from reorientations within the Church; some would share in the original Vaughan vision more fully than others; some would be more pastorally minded, and so on. Whatever the particular circumstances in which an Administrator found himself, and whatever particular gifts he brought to the office, he set the tone for the Cathedral and its mission.

Cardinal Vaughan's original Constitution established a number of officials to be responsible for various parts of the Cathedral's liturgy, all of them working under the Administrator. There was to be a Prefect of the Sacristy, responsible for everything belonging to the sacristy and the furniture of the Cathedral, and in charge of arranging the Masses and other services each week. He was responsible to the Master of Ceremonies. The latter was required to liaise with the Rector of the Choir School and with the Precentor, who was in charge of the Cathedral clergy when they were in choir and was required to see that everything there was performed correctly and devoutly. There was also the Master of Music, originally also given the title of Precentor. All these offices were to be filled by members of the Cathedral clergy – even the Master of Music, it seems, although when the constitution was issued Vaughan had already appointed a layman, Terry, to the post. It is not easy to see in every case where the responsibilities of one official ended and another's began; in practice one individual sometimes held more than one post, and this had been allowed for in the Constitution. It took time, of course, for the limits and extent of each job to become clear; in the early years there were rows over roles and overlapping jurisdictions. The requirements of running something as complex in its operations as the Cathedral could not all be worked out in advance, and there needed to be flexibility to allow for changing circumstances. A *modus vivendi* had to be established with the diocesan Council of Administration and, of course, with the Chapter – the fact that the Administrator was normally a canon helped here. All institutions can easily become hidebound; long service by officials can bring the benefits of continuity and experience, but it can also make innovation difficult. As will be seen, the Cathedral was not to avoid criticism on this score.

Such problems lay in the future. It is necessary to go back a few years, before the troubles over the choice of which priests should serve the Cathedral, to Vaughan's initial decision to build it. Once he had taken that decision, says his biographer, he wanted to start at once – and to finish as soon as possible. He would not be content to lay a foundation stone and then pass the burden of building on to succeeding generations. He wanted a cathedral that would be begun and made ready for use well within the ten years of active life he thought he could reasonably hope for.[13]

The most obvious obstacle to the realization of this 'a cathedral in our time' approach was financial. Could the English Catholics, even allowing for their increasing prosperity and standing, afford the necessary money? Vaughan apparently never doubted that he would be able to raise sufficient funds. There were some who feared that the Cardinal's desire not to load generations to come with a heavy financial burden might lead to the building of a cheap and unworthy Cathedral, run up, as they said, to suit a Cardinal in a hurry. None of the great cathedrals of the past had been built in a single generation, they claimed, and there was no reason why those who would benefit from having a cathedral in the future should not be expected to share the cost. Vaughan listened to all the critics but was not deterred.

Central to the solution of some of these problems was the issue of which architectural style the Cardinal would choose for his building. It was taken for granted by almost all who thought about it that the style would be some variation of Gothic, which had come to be accepted as the most suitable ecclesiastical style for the time; it expressed man's desire to reach up to God and it reminded a materialist age of a past time of faith; it also allowed some people to take refuge in medieval nostalgia instead of finding contemporary solutions to contemporary problems. The Cardinal shared many of these feelings for the past but he also knew that to build a Gothic cathedral of sufficient size would be both very expensive and very slow. He wanted something large and magnificent enough to be itself an act of worship to God, as well as being a fitting assertion of the Catholic presence in England. And it had to be completed and brought into use while he was still alive. He had in mind something on the lines of the Roman basilica churches – a building of which at least the shell could be built quickly. It was essential that he should choose the right architect.

NOTES

1   E. S. Purcell, *Life of Cardinal Manning, Archbishop of Westminster* (2 vols, 1895), II, pp. 354–5; Owen Chadwick, *The Victorian Church* (2 vols; 2nd ed, 1972), II, p. 242.
2   Purcell, II, pp. 354–5; J. G. Snead-Cox, *The Life of Cardinal Vaughan* (1912), II, pp. 314ff.; W. de l'Hopital, *Westminster Cathedral and Its Architect* (2 vols, 1919), I, ch. 2.
3   Purcell, II, p. 355; Snead-Cox, II, p. 318; de l'Hopital, I, pp. 14–17. Cardinal Vaughan owned *The Tablet* at this time. Vaughan was still pursuing Tatton Sykes in 1894 for a 'substantial donation'; Shane Leslie thought the problem was the would-be donor's chronic indecision – see his amusing footnote on p. 416 of his *Letters of Herbert Cardinal Vaughan to Lady Herbert of Lea* (1942).
4   Snead-Cox, II, p. 323.
5   *Guide to Westminster Cathedral* (1902), p. 25.
6   Snead-Cox, II, pp. 320, 327.

7 Snead-Cox, II, p. 346; de l'Hopital, II, p. 60.
8 The detailed story is told in R. Kollar, *Westminster Cathedral: From Dream to Reality* (Edinburgh, 1987).
9 Kollar, p. 116. Vaughan wrote later that he was 'entirely satisfied that it would be a most fatal step to have taken' to have employed the monks: see his letter to Mgr Dunn (29 March 1903) in AAW, V 1/21.
10 Kollar, p. 66.
11 *Constitution Dedicating and Endowing the College of Chaplains* (1902).
12 *The Tablet* (10 June 1933); in the event Bourne was too ill to attend and his sermon was read out.
13 Snead-Cox, II, p. 319.

Chapter 3

John Francis Bentley: architect and craftsman

VAUGHAN INITIALLY THOUGHT of organizing a competition to find the right architect: such competitions were popular at the time, perhaps because they seemed to fit in with prevailing notions of fair play and of the almost mystical belief that competition was nature's way of ensuring that the best would be produced. At one stage he was approached by a group of twelve Catholic architects asking to be allowed to submit their designs in this way. His initial enthusiasm, however, gave way when he learned that one particular architect, John Francis Bentley, would not consider entering any competition: he regarded them as completely unsatisfactory in what they produced and felt they demeaned the architect; as a friend said of him in this context, 'he disdained the honour of rivalry'. In the end the Cardinal dropped the idea of a competition and gave the commission to Bentley, admitting that the decision would cause 'many heartburnings'.[1]

John Bentley had been born in Doncaster in 1839, one of seventeen children of Ann and Charles Bentley, a successful wine merchant in the town. His interest in drawing and design had become evident at the time of the rebuilding of the parish church which had been destroyed by fire when Bentley was fourteen, but a suggestion that he might take up a career as an artist was rejected out of hand by his father; instead, he was apprenticed to a firm of builders. His skills as a draughtsman were so good, however, that he soon transferred to the office of Henry Clutton, a well-respected Catholic architect with a particular interest in the French Gothic style. As we have seen, Clutton was himself commissioned on a number of occasions by

Cardinal Manning to design the cathedral; his first design was long and narrow to suit the first site, his last was a vast Gothic building similar to St Patrick's in New York – 450 feet by 250 feet.[2]

While with Clutton Bentley did some work on the Jesuit church in Farm Street and on St Francis's, Notting Hill. He was offered a partnership in 1860 but decided instead to set up in practice on his own, although he was only 21. Thus began the slow building up of a reputation as an ecclesiastical architect. In 1862 he was received into the Catholic church by Cardinal Wiseman, being baptized in the new baptistery of St Francis's church which he had himself designed. To mark the occasion he took the name of Francis as a second Christian name. He obtained a number of Catholic commissions for minor works – for example, for Cardinal Manning's Oblates in Bayswater, and for a number of churches in Liverpool, including Bishop Eton and St Patrick's. He was later to design the new seminary at Hammersmith established by Cardinal Manning. Even when he became firmly established, however, he designed only a few complete churches – in all, four Catholic ones and one Anglican. He seemed to be better known as a designer of interior decorations, altars and stained glass, with a particular skill in wood and metal work.

In this context it may be noted that he became a member of the Art Workers' Guild, which had connections with the Arts and Crafts movement of the day; he was too much of an individualist, however, to share in the basic ideal of that movement which aimed at the collaboration of craftsmen and artists in the designing and making of works of art. He had also helped to found the Catholic Guild of St Gregory and St Luke, a mixed group of artists, antiquarians and theologians, which Bentley hoped would help to raise the low standard of Catholic church art and decoration by examining ancient Christian practice and setting out principles and guidelines. He soon became disappointed with the Guild and withdrew from membership – again, perhaps, because of the strong streak of individualism in his character. He never sought membership of such professional bodies as the Royal Institute of British Architects or the Architectural Association, and his daughter in her official biography wrote of his 'intellectually lonely and autocratic nature'.

It seems that some of Bentley's friend had been active in persuading the Cardinal that he would be the most suitable person for the job; he would also have known of the architect's work from what he had done for the Oblates and for Cardinal Manning. What seems to have persuaded the Cardinal most of all was that whenever he had asked those whom he was consulting for one name, they had collectively and individually named Bentley. There is an additional piece of evidence which is doubly revealing. About two weeks before the appointment was made a friend wrote to Bentley to say that the Cardinal was very taken with his decision to 'go and study the basilica in its own native haunts'.[3] This can only mean that, while the architect did not approach the Cardinal himself and offer his services, he was very interested in the outcome and was already taking steps to prepare himself for the work – or, at least, to show that he was willing to do so.

The remark is even more important in that it shows that word had got out as to the style of building that the Cardinal had in mind. In a private circular he had written of the old basilica of St Peter's in Rome, originally built in the fourth century by the Emperor Constantine, as the best model to follow. Most people had fully expected the style to be Gothic, in line with the taste and traditions of the Victorian age, and Bentley himself was undoubtedly a 'Gothic man' by predilection and training, though he had always shown an interest in the Romanesque buildings to be found in various parts of Europe. It was Vaughan who insisted on something completly different.

When it became known that the new building was not to be Gothic in style there was an immediate outcry; what, the critics asked, did the Cardinal mean by the 'basilican' style and what relevance could a church built in that style have to English Catholics? Would it not make them appear as un-English and alien as their detractors claimed they were? Surely, a cathedral in the grand style of English medieval architecture would highlight the essential links between present-day Catholicism and its glorious past in the great age of faith? And so it went on. The Cardinal, no matter how sure he was that his decision was the correct one, could not ignore such criticisms, for no cathedral at all could be built without the fundamental support of the laity.

He outlined his reasons in a letter to likely subscribers.[4] The first concerned the uses for which the cathedral was to be built: it had to provide enough space for a large congregation to have an uninterrupted view of the altar so that they could participate in the services; it should also allow them to see and hear the daily recitation of the Divine Office, which, as has been seen, was one of the Cardinal's main aims in building the Cathedral in the first place.

The second set of reasons were financial. He had no intention of building beyond the means available at any one time; at the same time, as we have seen, he wanted a building that could be completed in its basics within a reasonable period. Everyone agreed that a very large Gothic building would be both expensive and slow to build, whereas the proposed style would allow the shell to be completed quickly and brought into use – the decoration could then be added as money allowed, since it was not an intrinsic part of the structure as in a Gothic building. The wisdom of this line of argument may, perhaps, be illustrated by what happened to the Anglican cathedral in Liverpool; begun only a few years later in a Gothic style, it was not completed until 1978.

Thirdly, the Cardinal claimed that by avoiding the use of a Gothic style he would prevent comparisons between the new cathedral and Westminster Abbey just a short distance away. Such comparisons might have told against the Catholic body if their building turned out to be less grand than the Abbey, or it all might have seemed to be a presumptuous attempt to rival the Abbey on their part.

It was in this letter that the Cardinal first spoke publicly of a cathedral in the 'Christian Byzantine' style. It is little wonder that most of the Catholic body were mystified and would have preferred something familiar; it is difficult to be sure that even Vaughan himself had a clear idea of what the words meant – certainly, there were no examples in Western Europe that could be pointed to by way of explanation. As we have seen, he had in mind initially a building along the lines of the ancient basilicas which he knew so well from his years in Rome. Bentley's biographer claims that it was the architect who persuaded the Cardinal against the basilican style because of his own dislike of it; if it were not to be Gothic, then it should be something even older – hence the decision to go for a 'Christian Byzantine' style.

There had been something of a revival of artistic interest in Byzantine architecture and decoration since the middle of the century, along with a similar interest in the Romanesque styles of south-western France. The art critic Ruskin was influential here: he wrote admiringly of the older Italian churches, praising the multicoloured marbles and flat surfaces inside the buildings, and the use of colour outside. There was, he felt, an 'honesty' and simplicity in their construction; they were old, and Christian, and so a suitable alternative to Gothic for those who were tiring of the Gothic revival. The existence of an alternative to Gothic was welcomed by those in England who were involved in the Arts and Crafts movement. By the 1890s there existed a few examples of buildings in a Byzantine style in London. A Greek Orthodox cathedral had been built in Bayswater, designed by John Scott, son of the famous Gothic revivalist Sir George Gilbert Scott. The interior decoration of this cathedral was completed in 1893, and consisted of a mosaic covering of the dome and vaults, with the lower walls covered in marble. Probably the best known example of the 'new' style at the time was Cubitt's Union Chapel in Islington, built between 1875 and 1889 for the Congregationalists; here the architect set out to meet the needs of the congregation, and used as his basic design the square Greek cross. *The Builder* praised the approach, saying that a congregation which needed to be able to hear clearly would be better served by an 'area' than an 'avenue'; it claimed that Cubitt's inspiration had been the church of Santa Fosca in Torcello, near Venice, which Ruskin had praised so lavishly. Cubitt had, indeed, used the name 'Torcello' as his pseudonym in the competition for the chapel. Another admirer of the Byzantine style was the third Marquess of Bute, who had two churches built in it in Scotland; he and his son were to be generous patrons of Westminster Cathedral. Other artists involved in the revival were Robert Weir Schultz and Sidney Barnsley; both were connected with the Arts and Crafts movement and were to do work for the Cathedral.[5]

Cardinal Vaughan was not likely to have been impressed by references to a Greek Orthodox cathedral as a possible model – and, anyway, it was the wrong shape for a building which was to hold a large congregation. Still less would he have accepted a Congregational chapel. But perhaps Bentley found in the Cardinal a willing convert. He claimed later that what the Cardinal had wanted all along was to build what would be the principal church in England (Vaughan might have said, the Empire) in a style that was not confined to one country and which was 'absolutely primitive Christian'. This style, he argued, had been spread 'over many countries' up to the ninth century. Personally, he continued, he would have preferred a Gothic style, but on reflection he was inclined to think that the Cardinal had been right.[6] There was always in the Cardinal a desire to get back to a past when Christian values were uppermost in society and the evils of modern materialism had not appeared; if he could not imitate the Middle Ages then he would have to go back even further, to early Christian times.

Whatever the origins of the idea were, Bentley had already decided, as we have seen, that he would like to go to the Continent to study the early styles where they still existed; he planned to go mainly to Italy and then on to Constantinople; in the end he had to forgo the eastern part of the trip because of an outbreak of cholera. As far as we know he did not keep any notebooks or sketches of what he saw, but we can get some idea of what did and what did not impress him from a number of letters which he wrote while he was away, from November 1894 to March 1895.[7]

His first stop was Milan. Here he was not at all impressed by the heavily ornate Gothic cathedral, liking instead the older church of St Ambrose with its tall brick campanile, and the other ancient churches. At Pisa he found a detail which he had himself adopted in his earlier church of the Holy Rood in Watford: the continuation of the gallery arcade across the transepts so that the latter did not break the lines leading the eye to the sanctuary. It was claimed later that he had learned of this for the first time in Pisa, but his Watford church had been planned as early as 1879, and the same device had been used in St Augustine's, Kilburn, also from the 1870s. From Florence he wrote that the Duomo was 'architecturally, the worst large building I have ever seen', echoing in this the sentiments of Ruskin. He did, however, admire the famous baptistery and the fine campanile. When he got to Rome he was, again, largely unimpressed: it was full 'of a great number of dreadful churches', and he found it difficult to decide whether St Peter's or the Duomo was architecturally the worst large building which he had seen. Its effect was 'very fine, but produced at the sacrifice of scale'. Later he was to add St Paul's-outside-the-Walls to his list of architectural abominations. But Rome was not all loss: as the 'centre and keystone of Christian unity' he venerated the place more than he could say, and he spent a long time studying early Christian art and buildings as well as the great classical ruins.

It was when he left Rome and moved towards the north-east that his architectural interest was further stimulated. At Perugia there was the sixth-century circular church of San Angelo, and then there was Ravenna with its sixth-century churches of San Vitale, San Apollinare in Classe and San Apollinare Nuovo, and its famous baptisteries and other buildings. Ravenna was of particular interest because it was, as it were, the meeting point between East and West, having been at one time the Byzantine capital in Italy. One point of interest for him about these churches may well have been the fact that they were not of a single, 'pure' style: San Apollinare Nuovo, for example, was a basic Western-style basilica, but with enough Eastern features to make it quite different and much more impressive than such a basilica in Rome at the same period would have been.[8] Nor was it just the structure of these buildings that interested him; there were the magnificent early mosaics in both Greek and Roman styles, and beautifully carved capitals to the columns in San Vitale – something which he was to use to great advantage at Westminster. It was probably here that he realized the practical possibilities of using the Byzantine style by adapting it to modern needs. The very early churches were too small, having been built more with the needs of the liturgy than of the congregation in mind; yet they had a simplicity and a beauty which he had not seen elsewhere. When he got to

Venice and studied St Mark's in detail he saw what could be done: as he put it, the great cathedral showed what would have developed in the Byzantine style if the 'decadence of the Roman Empire' had not ended the growth of congregational needs in the East – it was, in a sense, moving in the right direction.[9] He also visited Torcello nearby: after such praise by Ruskin he could not have missed such an opportunity.

.While in Venice he was also studying a recently published definitive study of Santa Sophia in Constantinople, written by two English architects, Lethaby and Swainson. When his friends offered their sympathy that he had been unable to visit it in person, he replied that San Vitale at Ravenna and the book 'really told me all I wanted'. He returned home by way of Padua, Verona, Turin and Paris.

Without detailed notes and sketches it is impossible to say just which parts of all that he saw influenced him most when he came to draw the plans for his own cathedral. And one must not forget the influence of some of the great French cathedrals which he knew of already, especially, perhaps, those at Angoulême and Périgueux.[10] He certainly did not follow a single style, and nothing is to be gained by trying to attach a particular stylistic label to the finished building or finding his 'key' model. There are in it elements which remind the viewer of the Italian Renaissance, of Byzantine Ravenna and Constantinople and even of the dreaded Roman basilicas. As with all architects, he set out to solve a number of problems within the limitations imposed by the circumstances – the size and shape of the site, for example, the needs of the liturgy of the day and, of course, the restricted funds likely to be available. He was determined that the congregation should have an uninterrupted view of the high altar; that there should not be pillars or open transepts to distract the attention from that view; that there should not be a great dome, for that would demand open transepts and be another possible source of distraction; that the decoration of the interior of the building should be early Christian in inspiration; that the whole should be large enough to take a congregation of several thousands, and so on. His success, and his greatness, lay in producing a great building which meets these requirements and which has its own artistic unity. As has been said of Cubitt's Byzantine Union Chapel – it passes the prime architectural test: it works.[11]

On his return from Italy in March Bentley worked with remarkable speed. He produced two possible plans and obtained the Cardinal's general approval; he then prepared the site, so that the foundation stone could be laid on 29 June. This was done with great ceremonial before a crowd of

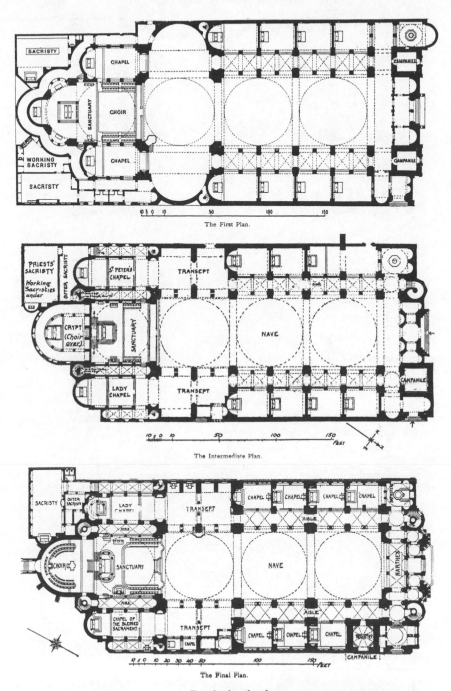

The First Plan.

The Intermediate Plan.

The Final Plan.

Developing the plan

These three drawings by Bentley show how the ground plan was altered: notice, for
example, the shape of the transepts and the change from two campaniles

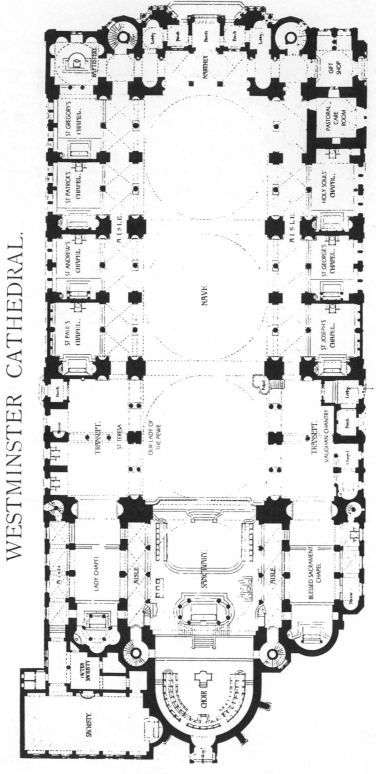

WESTMINSTER CATHEDRAL.

SACRISTY.

OUTER SACRISTY.

LADY CHAPEL.

AISLE.

SANCTUARY.

AISLE.

CHOIR.

BLESSED SACRAMENT CHAPEL.

Stair.

TRANSEPT.
ST TERESA.

OUR LADY OF THE PEWE.

TRANSEPT.
VAUGHAN CHANTRY.

Porch

Chapel

ST PAUL'S CHAPEL.

ST ANDREW'S CHAPEL.

ST PATRICK'S CHAPEL.

ST GREGORY'S CHAPEL.

BAPTISTERY.

ST JOSEPH'S CHAPEL.

ST GEORGE'S CHAPEL.

HOLY SOULS CHAPEL.

PASTORAL CARE ROOM.

GIFT SHOP.

AISLE.

AISLE.

NAVE.

AISLE.

AISLE.

NARTHEX.

Lady

Porch

Porch

Porch

Lady

Chapel

Porch

13. Jam St. Adelphi. 1895

several thousands, including the usual dignitaries and representatives of foreign countries. The Cardinal was convinced that nothing could now prevent his vision from becoming a reality, even money; as he announced to the crowds, the generosity of those who had responded to his 'few very simple letters' meant that he had in hand £75,000 towards the building.[12]

Bentley worked to clarify his ideas and refine his plans. There were constructional issues, too – he wanted to avoid the use of iron in the structure, for example, since he regarded it as 'a source of decay', though there is some used as ties in the transepts. Those who are expert in these matters speak of Bentley's great engineering and constructional abilities, and of the overall 'audacity' of his building in this regard.[13] What is particularly striking to the lay person's eye, perhaps, is the great size of the main arches in each of the bays of the nave, and how the space within these is broken by smaller ones, so that a pattern of arches is built up from floor to dome, with the shapes of the arches repeated in the windows. The plain brick finish of these massive vaults and arches, and their size, is more reminiscent of some of the ruins of Classical Rome than of the early Christian churches which Bentley had studied.

Shortly after the laying of the foundation stone he wrote to a friend to say how glad he was that the Basilica and Italian styles had been 'cast aside'; what he intended was not to create a new style, for that would be impossible, but to develop as far as he could the 'first phase of Christian architecture'. A few years later, when he was starting to design the Archbishop's house he said that it would be in character with the Cathedral, but what that was he did not know, except that it was done from what he had seen 'in the East'; at the same time he had not seen anything like it. In answering the critics at this time he agreed that the cathedral would be un-English, but nothing like as un-English as 'modern Gothic with its stained and varnished work, and many other abominations'. Although he always worked on his own and was uninfluenced by movements and fashions, he showed that he was thinking along the same lines as some of his forward-looking contemporaries, such as Norman Shaw. He was, he said, getting 'quite tired of Antiquarian Architecture': while it was the business of a student to copy and study ancient work, that had to cease once he attached his own name to a piece of work; copying would not be tolerated in literature, sculpture, painting or music, so why should it be in architecture?[14]

His last defence of what he had been trying to do was written for the first *Guide to the Cathedral*, published in 1902. The style was 'early Christian Byzantine', he wrote, but the building would be unique in Western Europe.

'Byzantine' should not, however, be confused with what was 'generally and loosely called the Basilica style, as for instance the new church of Montmartre in Paris, or the Romanesque style . . . in Italy and Spain'. The style of the new Cathedral, he went on, would be the same as that of Santa Sophia in Constantinople; in no sense of the word could it be called Italian – the nearest Italian examples would be St Mark's, Venice, and San Vitale, in Ravenna. Clearly, Bentley remained very sensitive to accusations that his building would be Italianate; the word Italian had been attached insultingly to English Catholics for too long for him to be able to ignore it. It is clear, too, from this defence that English Catholics themselves were still looking for his 'model', for something to compare his work with; perhaps because they had been used for so long to the second-rate and the imitation they could hardly believe that they had at last been given a unique masterpiece.

On the whole Bentley and the Cardinal found it easy to agree on these matters, which was just as well as Bentley had little regard for the artistic abilities of the clergy and normally refused to accept any interference on their part in architectural questions.[15] The Cardinal was, perhaps, being naïve when he claimed that, having laid down certain conditions as to size, space, chapels and style, he 'left the rest to him'. Bentley did not have quite the free hand implied. It is clear, for example, that it was Vaughan who insisted on one campanile instead of the two Bentley had planned, and he continued to offer 'suggestions': all inscriptions were to be submitted to experts in Rome; would not golden glass in the dome given a warm effect? Norwegian red granite would make the best steps for the entrance and the chapels, and so on. It seems that Bentley was able to ignore much of this, but on occasion he was angered by the Cardinal's actions. In order not to offend a wealthy benefactor the Cardinal accepted the gift of an Italian marble pulpit which was out of keeping with Bentley's ideas. He also accepted from some of the English bishops the gift of a throne which was an exact replica of the papal throne in the Lateran, and against which Bentley protested in vain. One can understand both the Cardinal's dilemma and Bentley's remonstrances; perhaps the latter was lucky that the age-old frictions between patron and artist were not more troublesome.

The Cardinal continued to take a very detailed interest in everything to do with the Cathedral. One example may be given here. After Bentley's death he corresponded with Christian Symons, the artist chosen to paint the great crucifix that was to hang over the high altar. His concerns were much wider than those of cost. He sent Symons a photograph of a picture of the face of Christ which he had found particularly impressive; he insisted that the image

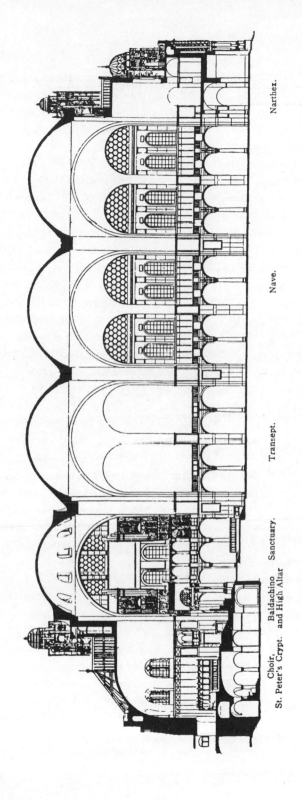

Choir,   Baldachino   Sanctuary.   Transept.   Nave.   Narthex.
St. Peter's Crypt.   and High Altar

Longitudinal section

Bentley's drawing shows the pattern of arches which is such a striking feature of
the building

must be of the live Christ – there must be no pierced side, but there could be a crown of thorns; the body must be seen to *hang*. He suggested the quotations from the *Stabat Mater* which should go on the ends of the cross, and the painting which should appear on the reverse side. He was not one for choosing an artist and letting him or her get on with it.[16]

Once building began progress was rapid, though Vaughan was being unreasonably optimistic in hoping that it would be finished in time for the celebrations of the golden jubilee of the Restoration of the Hierarchy in September 1900! By October 1896 the foundations were completed up to ground level, and a new contract was signed for the superstructure up to the domes and vaulting. It was typical of Vaughan's caution that separate contracts should be signed for each major part of the construction, and that the builders should be paid fortnightly for the work completed: he was determined not to allow any debt to build up. He expected Bentley to produce detailed estimates of the cost of each new stage of building, and requests for these arrived on the architect's desk every few months; when they were not immediately forthcoming the Cardinal became impatient and Bentley became annoyed – as Vaughan said, 'Mr Bentley was a poet . . . he cared little for economy'.[17] He was being fairer to his architect when he said that he had a passionate concern for detail; if financial estimates were delayed it was because Bentley was already working impossible hours to complete every aspect of the building plans, including the decoration and furnishings.

It is surprising that while there were a few delays caused by labour problems and shortages of materials, there were none caused by shortages of funds. Even when the monthly outgoings amounted to almost £2,500 in 1898, and the subscriptions amounted to only £1,000 a month, the work was able to be continued. Vaughan did not achieve his aim of leaving a debt-free building to his successor (when he died in 1903 the sum outstanding on the building itself was £16,000), but he was remarkably successful all the same. He issued few appeals, but when he did he was able to find the appropriate phrases which somehow won the approval of those able to respond: he caught the contemporary mood of Catholic nostalgia for a lost age of faith and conversionist zeal for the present, with a nice pinch of national and imperial sentiment to complete the recipe. In his first appeal he wrote that the Empire should 'possess in its very centre a living example of the beauty and of the majesty of the worship of God, rendered by solemn daily choral monastic service, as in the olden time within the walls of Canterbury, during a thousand years . . . We desire that, at least in this immense capital

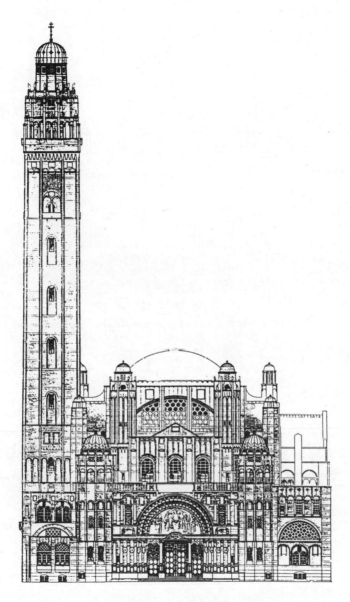

The completed west front

SCALE ⟨scale bar⟩ OF FEET.

Bentley's drawing of the east elevation

of a world-wide empire of power and influence, in this great commercial mart of human industry, there should arise without delay a cathedral fully presenting the cosmopolitan faith and devotion of the Catholic Church.'[18]

Whenever possible Vaughan preferred to appeal to individuals rather than to make general appeals to the Catholic body, since he was sensitive to the financial demands continually being made on the latter for new parishes and schools. There was also the question of how far a national appeal would have been successful, for while he had no doubt that the Cathedral would become a national shrine and a symbol of English Catholicism's growing presence in the country, such developments lay in the future and northern Catholics in particular might not have been moved to be generous in what must have seemed to many a purely diocesan cause. The other English bishops did launch an appeal in 1899, when work on the domes and vaults was about to start, and the parish collections brought in a useful but not all that impressive £3,500.

In those days of openly published subscription lists to every sort of good cause, the Cardinal had no compunction in offering to substantial donors both spiritual benefits and some lasting publicity. Three groups of benefactors were to have their names remembered in a special *Liber Vitae* which was to be 'honoured according to ancient usage'. They were, first of all, those who gave at least £1,000 to the building fund: these were given the title of Founder of Westminster Cathedral, and their names were to be inscribed on a special plaque to be placed in the main entrance; they were to have a monthly Mass said for them for ever and a special Requiem every November. The second group were the Special Benefactors, who had given or collected not less than £300 within three years. They shared in the annual Requiem Mass. Finally, there were the Named Benefactors who gave not less than £10; they shared in a general written request in the sacristy that a special memento be made in all Masses said in the cathedral for all Founders and Benefactors. Full lists of all subscriptions, large and small, were published in the *Westminster Cathedral Record* which appeared inter-mittently between 1896 and 1902.[19]

A list published in 1919 of those who had become Founders since 1894 gives 101 names or initials, and adds 'and several anonymous donors'. The total sum raised in this way must have been very substantial as many gave more than the minimum: the Duke of Norfolk gave £10,000, Lord Brampton £3,000, Lady Brampton over £2,000, a Miss Dodsworth nearly £6,500, and Vaughan himself £5,000. In addition, Baroness Weld bequeathed over £11,000, which was used for the Lady Chapel. While the old Catholic families are prominent, along with some more recent converts from the nobility and gentry, the length of the lists (especially if one includes the many who gave £100 or more but did not merit the title of Founder) is testimony to the solid strength of the Catholic middle classes at the time – and also to the attractiveness of the idea of at last having a worthy cathedral.

Three other major attempts to raise funds may be mentioned here. In 1896 the Chairman of the Executive Committee, Mgr Fenton (later to be the first Administrator of the Cathedral, and made Bishop of Amycla as Auxiliary to Cardinal Bourne in 1904) went to Italy and collected a large sum in Rome and Florence – the Pope himself, Leo XIII, became a Founder. Fenton tried to get a collection organized in France, in memory of the help given to the French émigrés to England a century before, but unfortunately approached the head of the French ex-royal family, who tried to make it a purely family affair but had done nothing by the time of his death.[20]

Then there was the Cardinal's eccentric brother, Fr Kenelm Vaughan. He took on the task of organizing the subscriptions for the Blessed Sacrament chapel, and travelled around Spain begging from rich and poor. He bestowed the fanciful title of 'Fundadores del Sagrario' ('Founders of the Tabernacle') on those who gave more than £50. The Archbishop of Seville became a Founder and the Royal Family also subscribed. In two years he collected almost £4,000. He then followed in his brother's footsteps and moved to South America, where the Cardinal had gone in the 1860s to collect for his missionary foundation and had raised £11,000. Kenelm was there for nine years and when he returned he had collected a total of over £18,000 'from the Spanish races' for the chapel and its upkeep. He died two years later, in 1909. Surely he deserves, if anyone does, to be named among the Founders of Westminster Cathedral.

Thirdly, donors were invited from time to time to give enough money for particular pieces or features of the building, and the 'prices' of these were published in the *Record*. A marble column could cost between £50 and £150, depending on whether it was a large one in the nave or a much smaller one in the crypt or tribune; 10,000 bricks could be paid for by a donation of £33; the special columns of the baldacchino over the high altar cost £250 each; the Stations of the Cross cost £75 each (the donors got Eric Gill's sculpted ones instead of the tiled ones they had subscribed for – surely a bargain?). Again, the approach was very successful and almost every item had its cost covered in this way.

Much of the credit for the general fund-raising in these years must go the treasurer of the Building Fund, Mgr Canon William Johnson. He had spent almost all his priestly life as secretary to Cardinal Manning, and he took on the role of fund-raiser with enthusiasm. He was later appointed Vicar General and then, in 1906, auxiliary bishop. The issues of the *Cathedral Record* give the results of his efforts: over £13,000 was collected in the six months to December 1900, with another £7,000 in the next sixteen months. He had a turnstile installed in 1899, and charged people 6d to view the building: in this way another £3,000 was raised in eighteen months. By the end of 1902 nearly £150,000 had been received or promised in general subscriptions. An additional £48,000 was received from the Charity Commissioners for the sale of the Moorfields site.[21]

At the time of the laying of the foundation stone in 1895 it had been estimated that £140,000 would be needed for fees and to complete the main structure; in addition, there was a mortgage on the land of £20,000. By 1898 the mortgage was still there, and over £88,000 had been spent on fees, labour and materials; four years later the mortgage had been paid off (with the money from the Charity Commissioners), but a further £16,000 was needed before all the debts could be cleared and the essential work on the structure completed. The Cardinal made this the object of his last appeal in June 1902: he hoped that everything could be paid off so that the cathedral could be consecrated. He called for a 'last effort, a last sacrifice', but it was to be some years before his successor could claim that everything was ready for the consecration which took place in 1910, by which time over £253,000 had been spent.[22]

Vaughan had originally hoped to open the cathedral to mark the golden jubilee of the Restoration of the Hierarchy, in 1900. By early 1902 he was hoping to be able to have the opening coincide with the coronation of the new king – no doubt to add an international flavour to the proceedings. Again, essential work was not completed in time. In the end the cathedral was never officially opened but rather crept into use: the Divine Office was sung for the first time in May 1902, but in the hall, not the cathedral proper. In June that year a concert was held in the main building in the presence of the Cardinal and about three thousand people. It was not until early in 1903 that Mass was said regularly in the cathedral – first of all in the Lady Chapel, which then served as a parish church with daily Mass, until the rest of the building was opened for public use on Christmas Eve of the same year.[23]

Bentley, unfortunately, did not live to see any of this. He had had a slight stroke in 1898 but had continued to work as hard as ever; a second stroke in 1901 slowed him down, but still he was busy designing the intricate marble floor which he had planned for the whole cathedral, and the marble covering for the walls of the nave and sanctuary. (He was very disappointed when the decision was taken to put in a wood-block floor instead, on grounds both of economy and of the English climate.) He died suddenly in March 1902, on the day before his nomination for the highly prized Gold Medal of the Royal Institute of British Architects was to be confirmed. The knowledge that he was to be nominated for it had given him considerable satisfaction, for he valued, as he wrote to a friend, the judgement of those who were 'endeavouring to make architecture a living, not a dead, art'.[24] The criticisms, of course, continued. They ranged from harmless cracks about the Cardinal's 'railway station', and about the 'Roman candle' of a campanile, to the more serious remarks of those who still hankered after a Gothic building. Perhaps foremost among these were the biographers of Ambrose Phillipps de Lisle, E. S. Purcell and Edwin de Lisle; while with hindsight one can read their outpourings with amusement, at the time they were taken all the more seriously because they seemed to be writing with authority and, in particular, with an inside knowledge of what Cardinal Manning had wanted. (Purcell was Manning's official biographer.) They attacked the lack of continuity with 'our glorious old Catholic English Gothic', and described the cathedral as a 'sort of pre-Heptarchical evolution – Byzantino-Babylonian, bizarre . . . a megalomaniac hulk in a sea of unsightliness'. They claimed that there had been a conspiracy in the 'circle' responsible for the design to keep hidden from the public Manning's wishes, and also claimed that the Pope himself had wondered why Bentley had been sent to Bulgaria or Dalmatia for his models instead of to Yorkshire which was 'so rich in sacred architectural memories'.[25] The continued sniping perhaps made it easier for those who, after Bentley's death, wished to move away from his plans and designs to something 'more acceptable' to the people.

The Cardinal, of course, had nothing but praise for his architect when he preached at the funeral. Bentley, he said, was the ideal architect for any work that was 'to excel in artistic beauty'. He was no mere copyist, or slave to tradition; whatever he produced was stamped with his own individuality; it was alive and original, and he had a genius for taking infinite pains with detail. He was not ambitious to get on, the Cardinal claimed, nor was he self-assertive – but he coveted to do well. This last phrase of the Cardinal is important. It will be clear from what has been written in this chapter that Bentley had little patience with the 'antiquarians'; he did, however, value the views of fellow professionals, as we have seen over the RIBA nomination. He had been delighted when he had been able to show the distinguished architect, Norman Shaw, and the architectural historian,

Professor W. R. Lethaby, over the site and they had responded very positively. Lethaby's praise and subsequent writing in favour of the cathedral is not too surprising – he had done more than anyone to revive an interest in Byzantine architecture, and he had been the co-author of the book on Santa Sophia which Bentley had relied on.[26]

Shaw's praise was equally warm-hearted. When there was a proposal later to hold a competition for the design of the Anglican cathedral in Liverpool he objected strongly: they should choose an architect and let him get on with it. This, he claimed, had been what had happened at Westminster, and 'see what the result is! Beyond all doubt the finest church that has been built for centuries. Superb in its scale and character, and full of the most devouring interest, it is impossible to overrate the magnificence of this design. It is like a revelation after the feeble Gothic stuff on which we have been mainly fed for the last half-century.' Shaw's biographer adds that, hyperbole apart, most other architects agreed with Shaw.[27] A recent architectural historian has said that it is hard to overrate its impact in the years after its opening, an impact which was felt by Nonconformists as much as by anyone. When, for example, a new Congregationalist church was opened near Lytham in Lancashire in 1912 it was described as a 'dignified example of Byzantine architecture . . . a sister, though a small one, to Westminster Roman Catholic Cathedral'.[28]

The Cardinal did not outlive his architect by very long, dying only a little over a year after Bentley, in June 1903; his funeral was the first solemn event celebrated in the cathedral – in a sense, its official opening. Criticized by historians for his closeness to Manning and an excessive devotion to all things Roman, for an apparent remoteness from worldly issues (an inheritance, perhaps, from his recusant background), and for a triumphalism of which his grandiose plans for a great cathedral are seen as proof, it is difficult to give a balanced summary of Vaughan's achievements. What can be said here is that for a man who was also criticized as having no interest in literature or the arts, he did remarkably well in choosing Bentley as his architect and Terry as his first Master of Music. His successor, Cardinal Bourne, was clear about what he had achieved: 'Has there within the last hundred years been a single bishop or priest in England who could have contemplated such an enterprise, and not turned from it in dismay? . . . (he) made it possible to carry out in this great capital of the Empire the full liturgy of the Catholic Church.'[29] Vaughan had always insisted that what he wanted was a 'live' cathedral, used every day to give praise to God and bring spiritual benefit to the people. Bentley had shared this vision – and his building was a conspicuous and successful contribution towards the realization of their shared ideal.

By the time Vaughan died in June 1903, the building of the Cathedral was complete in all its essentials and had been opened to the public. He had set up the administration to see that it was well organized and could perform its functions. An essential part of his ideal had begun to be realized when the Divine Office had been sung there for the first time on 7 May 1902. To have got so far with limited resources in only eight years since the laying of the foundation stone had been a truly tremendous achievement. Of course, problems remained in the way of realizing his vision to the full – perhaps the most intractable being the need to imbue a body made up of English secular clergy with a feeling of warmth for a choral vocation. There was also the question of the decoration of the interior of the building, which was to cause Cardinal Bourne as much worry as anything else, and the need to establish a choir school and create a musical tradition. And there were, it almost goes without saying, ever recurring financial problems.

There was no formal opening of the Cathedral. After Vaughan's funeral the next event was the enthronement of Cardinal Bourne in 1903, followed by the opening of the building to the public for daily use on Christmas Eve of the same year. It very soon became the setting for a number of national and international Catholic events – the celebration of the centenary of St Gregory the Great in 1904, the international Eucharistic Congress in 1908, the celebration of the eighth centenary of St Anselm of Canterbury in 1909 and of the diamond jubilee of the Restoration of the Hierarchy in England and Wales in 1910. This last event took place at the same time as the consecration of the Cathedral, and was attended by three archbishops, twenty bishops, eight abbots and hundreds of clergy; amongst the lay dignitaries present were the Catholic Lord Mayor of London, Sir John Knill, and other mayors from around the country, members of the nobility and many of the Founders of the Cathedral. The consecration was itself a considerable achievement, for it meant that the building was free of debt (a requirement before any church can be consecrated). Bourne had launched a special appeal in January 1910, for donations to pay off the final £7,000 that was still owing, and this was done in time for the consecration to take place in the June. So from the laying of the foundation stone to the consecration took only fifteen years, longer than Vaughan had originally hoped but very much shorter than could reasonably have been foreseen.[30]

The outstanding event in these years, however, was the holding of the Eucharistic Congress in 1908. International Eucharistic Congresses were held every year, normally in a Catholic country, and were solemn occasions for public displays of devotion to the Blessed Sacrament with street processions, special Masses, open air Benedictions, sermons and lectures. None had ever been held in an English-speaking country, and that such an event should have been held in London at all was an acknowledgement of the growing strength and status of the English Catholic body. It did not pass off without incident. At the last moment the government gave in to Protestant pressure and forbade the carrying of the Blessed Sacrament in the outdoor procession for fear of the riots which had been threatened; apparently the Cardinal had had his own misgivings about this but had been persuaded by the Congress Committee to allow the procession to be planned. So late was the government's decision to impose a ban that it was only announced to those attending the Congress on the day before the procession. When it did take place, without the Blessed Sacrament, it appears that there was some trouble from hostile crowds at points along the route – at the junction of Carlisle Place and Francis Street, in Rochester Row and Greycoat Place, and there were fears at one stage for the safety of the Papal Legate, Cardinal Vannutelli. The report of these minor outbreaks of hostility came in eyewitness accounts written long after the event; at the time no mention was made of them in *The Tablet*'s account at all, while *The Times* reported that everything had passed off without any disturbance or serious unpleasantness.

The Congress was voted to have been a great success; it received widespread notice in the national press (as did the consecration two years later), with extensive pictorial coverage. On the whole the national papers praised the tact and diplomacy of Bourne and condemned the weakness of the government in giving in to the Protestant extremists. It must have seemed to the Cardinal the realization of Vaughan's vision of the Cathedral as the centre and showpiece of English Catholicism and the focus of the Catholic world.[31]

NOTES

1 W. de l'Hopital, *Westminster Cathedral and Its Architect* (2 vols, no date, but 1919) is the best source for biographical detail about Bentley. Mrs de l'Hopital was Bentley's daughter and also worked as his secretary. Her work is very detailed and useful, if rather uncritical.

2 B. Little, *Catholic Churches Since 1623* (1966).

3 De l'Hopital, I, pp. 22–3.

4 J. G. Snead-Cox, *The Life of Cardinal Vaughan* (1912), II, pp. 328–9.

5 C. Binfield, 'A chapel and its architect: James Cubitt and Union Chapel, Islington, 1874–1889' in *The Church and the Arts*, ed. D. Wood (Oxford, 1992). See also R. Dixon

and S. Muthesius, *Victorian Architecture* (1978), and G. Stamp and C. Amery, *Victorian Buildings of London* (1980), pp. 128–9.

6   De l'Hopital, I, p. 25.
7   De l'Hopital. See also the excellent edition of Bentley's letters by Peter Howell in *Architectural History: Journal of the Society of Architectural Historians of Great Britain*, vol. 23 (1980) and vol. 25 (1982). It is worth noting that Vaughan was also in Rome at this time, from January to March/April 1895; we can only assume that he and Bentley discussed the future Cathedral at some length.
8   R. Krautheimer, *Early Christian and Byzantine Architecture* (1965), pp. 196–8.
9   *Cathedral Record* (January 1896).
10 B. Fletcher, *A History of Architecture* (16th edn, 1956), pp. 253, 293, 300, 863.
11 Binfield, p. 444.
12 De l'Hopital. See ch. I for full description of the occasion. For the inscription on the stone and the dedication, see Appendix 2, p. 154 below.
13 A. Derrick, *The Tablet* (8 May 1982), pp. 449–50; de l'Hopital, *passim*.
14 Bentley to Hadfield (5 July 1895, 16 January and 4 February 1899) in Howell, vol. 25 (1982), pp. 81, 84. The reference to Shaw is also on p. 85.
15 AAW, Cathedral File I, Bentley and Marshall letters, Bentley to Symons (30 May 1891).
16 Snead-Cox, II, pp. 343–45, for Cardinal and Bentley; for Cardinal and Symons, AAW, as in previous note (22 February 1902).
17 Snead-Cox, II, pp. 342, 345.
18 Quoted in de l'Hopital, I, p. 260.
19 Financial details in de l'Hopital, I, ch. XI, and Snead-Cox, II. The *Westminster Cathedral Record* was planned to appear quarterly, but only eleven issues were published; from 1898 it was published as an occasional special supplement to *The Tablet*. Its successor, the *Westminster Cathedral Chronicle*, first appeared in January 1907, and lasted until 1967. It has been followed by the *News Sheet*, the *Westminster Cathedral Journal*, and the current *Westminster Cathedral Bulletin*.
20 De l'Hopital, I, pp. 263–4.
21 Snead-Cox, II, pp. 339–40. The redundant church of St Mary, Moorfields, was sold in 1899.
22 Appeal reprinted in *Guide to Westminster Cathedral* (1902), p. 54.
23 De l'Hopital, I, pp. 268–9. For the concert, *The Tablet* (14 June 1902), p. 940. What is now the Lady Chapel was originally planned to be the Blessed Sacrament Chapel and vice versa. The change around was made so that processions from the sacristy would not have to pass through or in front of the Blessed Sacrament Chapel on their way to the High Altar; when the change was made is not clear.
24 De l'Hopital, II, pp. 668–9.
25 De l'Hopital, I, p. 308; E. S. Purcell and E. de Lisle, *Life and Letters of Ambrose Phillips de Lisle* (2 vols, 1900), II, pp. 212–13.
26 De l'Hopital, I, p. 308.
27 A. Saint, *Richard Norman Shaw* (1976), pp. 218–19.
28 J. C. G. Binfield, 'The White Church, Fairhaven: an artist trader's Protestant Byzantium', *Transactions of the Historic Society of Lancashire and Cheshire*, vol. 142 (1993), pp. 155ff.
29 E. Oldmeadow, *Francis Cardinal Bourne* (2 vols, 1940, 1944), I, pp. 219–20.
30 De l'Hopital, I, pp. 317ff.; *Chronicle* (1910), pp. 218–23.
31 *Chronicle* (1908); *The Tablet* in Oldmeadow, I, pp. 380–2; reminiscences of Mgr J. Collings, *Chronicle* (1956), pp. 20–1.

Chapter 4

Music in the Cathedral:
the first fifty years

THE SINGING of the full Divine Office and of the Mass every day as the Church's official worship of God began in the Cathedral in 1902 and has continued without a break until the present day. If the performance of this liturgy were to be maintained at the highest standard, the Cathedral authorities would have to develop a choir with the musical expertise to match the best in the country. This involved the establishment of a residential Choir School to provide the trained boys' voices, and the employment of a body of full-time professional singers, both of which were unknown in English Catholic cathedrals at the time. Here, again, the achievement was outstanding, and within a few years the music at the Cathedral was the talk of London's musical circles and the Cathedral's reputation spread throughout Europe. Two factors were all-important in this initial success. The first was that a new approach to Catholic church music was being developed as the result of a revolutionary document issued by the Pope, St Pius X. The second was the appointment of an outstanding first Master of Music at the Cathedral whose ideas about the type of music best suited to Catholic churches were already developing along similar lines.

The Pope published his reforms in November 1903, by means of a *Motu Proprio*.[1] He set out to do away with the abuses which he felt had led to the decline of sacred music over the previous two or three hundred years, and to return to the simplicity of the Church's earlier tradition. He condemned the theatrical style of singing that had become common, especially in larger churches, where the music was a performance for the congregation to listen

51

to and often interfered with the proper carrying out of the liturgy. He referred, in particular, to the Viennese school of music as being unsuitable for use in the liturgy. The ideal style of sacred music was, according to the Pope, the ancient Gregorian chant, or plainsong, which had a simplicity and a beauty which was unsurpassed by any other style. While this should have pride of place in Catholic churches, it was also acceptable to use the polyphonic style of music of the sixteenth and early seventeenth centuries as expressed above all in the sacred works of such composers as Palestrina and Victoria.

One of the advantages which the Pope saw in plainsong was that it could be taught to ordinary congregations. In that way the people could be encouraged to join in the music at Mass and other liturgical celebrations and would cease to be merely an audience. The Pope ordered the setting up of diocesan commissions to oversee the music in Catholic churches and to establish lists of what would be acceptable in them. In that way the decorum due in the house of God would be maintained, and the music would serve to enhance the words of the liturgy instead of obscuring them. While the Pope had much to say against the current practices in church music, he was not against either modern music at its best or national differences in the forms used. He was, however, opposed to any vernacular singing during solemn liturgical functions.

There had been a movement within the Church for some years to revive plainsong and to encourage its adoption as the principal form of sacred music. Its adherents saw many advantages in this, but perhaps best of all was the fact that it was so unlike secular music as to leave no doubt that what was being sung was different, was sacred: it had an air of mysticism and of remote beauty. The revival, in so far as it was widespread enough to warrant the word, was strongest in France and Germany in a number of Benedictine houses, and especially at Solesmes, where considerable research was undertaken to establish the authentic plainsong tradition – a number of competing styles and interpretations had grown up over the centuries. In England the cause had been taken up especially by the Benedictine nuns at Stanbrook, and Pius X himself had been one of the first to recognize their efforts for the restoration of the authentic form of church music.[2]

The Catholic Church in England had, perhaps, escaped the worst excesses of nineteenth-century music, partly because few churches had the resources to employ large choirs and there were few fashionable churches. Yet it had not escaped altogether and there were parish churches where a handful of untrained singers murdered Mozart's masses; and there were a few churches

A view along the north side of the building (Ambrosden Avenue). The poster on the
hoarding advertises the first London performance of Elgar's *Dream of Gerontius* (1903)

Sir Richard Runciman Terry, Master of
Music 1901–24

Cardinal Francis Bourne, Archbishop of
Westminster 1903–35

Terry receives the
congratulations of his
choirboys in 1922 on the
occasion of his knighthood

The choir in 1905: this is the oldest known photograph of the full choir. Terry is
seated centre (with nautical beard). The boy standing fourth from left in the third
row from the front is Lancelot Long, who succeeded Terry as Choir Master

Aerial view of the Cathedral: the picture shows how hemmed in the building
was before the opening to Victoria Street was made. Photo: Aerofilms

large enough to ape their Continental cousins – Brompton Oratory, for example, where it was considered suitable for Good Friday to have a full performance of Tchaikovsky's 'Pathétique' symphony. At another level, when Cardinal Bourne visited St Patrick's, Soho, in 1904 he had to forbid the use of an orchestra of fiddles and cornets at a 'grand' High Mass.[3]

When Cardinal Vaughan was faced with the question of who should be appointed as Master of Music in the Cathedral these papal pronouncements were still two years in the future. By a happy chance, however, he chose someone who was already thinking along similar lines: Richard (later Sir Richard) Runciman Terry, then in charge of music at Downside. Terry had started his musical career at King's College, Cambridge, where he had been choral scholar. He had become a Catholic in 1896, and, on becoming choir master at Downside, had begun to revive the tradition of sixteenth-century Catholic church music, introducing into the choir's repertoire works by both Continental and English composers. He took his choir to Ealing to sing at the opening of the new Benedictine church, where they performed a Mass by Byrd, and motets by Palestrina, Philips and Allegri. The Cardinal was the preacher for the occasion, and on hearing the choir, he determined that he would have Terry as his Master of Music at the new Cathedral. The appointment turned out to be of crucial importance, and not just for the Cathedral. It gave Terry a national platform in London and he quickly established the Cathedral as a centre of musical excellence, and led the way in the country in reviving sixteenth-century English and Continental religious music. His time at the Cathedral was marked by frustrations and tensions, not all of them of others' making, but if Bentley had been an inspired choice by the Cardinal as architect, the same could be said of the choice of Terry as Master of Music.[4]

Terry has been described as part impresario, part artist and part scholar. He could spend days deciphering manuscripts in the Bodleian, Oxford, or in the British Museum, to bring back into use a forgotten composition by a little-known English composer of the fifteenth or sixteenth century, and he became the country's leading expert on the sacred music of composers such as Tallis and Byrd, bringing about a genuine renaissance of forgotten or lost treasures. For all his standing in these areas, however, he was never interested in an academic approach to music; whatever he did was geared to increasing the repertoire of music available for church use. Music publishers despaired of getting manuscripts from him on time, or even at all, and he was usually too impatient to get pieces performed to bother with full transcriptions. As long as there was enough for the choir to sing from he was satisfied, and his boys could find themselves copying out their own parts instead of doing 'lines' for punishment. Nor was he an élitist: his interest in carols and vernacular hymns shows that there was a genuinely popular side to him, and he was concerned to get ordinary parish choirs working properly and wrote a number of works to assist them. He had a very strong Catholic faith, and an instinctive understanding of the role of the liturgy and of music within it: sacred music was to adorn, to assist, to elevate, but never to dominate.

The daily liturgy meant that the choir required a very large repertoire of hundreds of Masses and motets. In 1910, for example, no fewer than 420 solemn High Masses were sung in the Cathedral. The wealth of sixteenth-century compositions was an obvious source for such a repertoire, especially as that particular style of polyphonic music had won the approbation of Rome because of its supposed closeness to the beauty of plainsong. Terry mixed English and Continental composers to produce a genuinely international repertoire, which was heard at its best in the services of Holy Week – the peak of the year's musical activity for the choir. In 1910, for example, no fewer than 40 Spanish works were to be heard in Holy Week, alongside works by Tallis, Palestrina, Byrd, Mundy, Terry himself and others – and, of course, a large amount of plainsong. Terry's own favourite among his English discoveries seems to have been Taverner whom he regarded as the biggest find of all; he devoted much of his energies to making the music known and performed, and in 1921 Holy Week in the Cathedral was described as a 'Taverner festival', with five of the composer's Masses sung by the choir.[5]

It was not surprising that London's music critics soon realized that in the Cathedral they had a new and unusual source of first-class music. By 1906 *The Daily Telegraph* was describing the choir as 'one of the most beautiful choirs in Europe'; in 1907, commenting on Holy Week, the same paper said 'There comes to a close a week that represented well nigh a best possible in the rendering of church music, and had presented many great specimens of the world's musical literature'. *The Times* regularly reviewed the music at the Cathedral, and the more specialist musical press was full of praise for what Terry was achieving. What did that early choir sound like? There is a remarkable 1909 recording of the men of the choir singing a Palestrina Mass (the BBC broadcast the *Gloria* from it in 1993). If it comes across as rather unsubtle, one has to remember that the recording was made before the advent of electric recordings, and made by the men standing around a large horn and singing as strongly as possible. Later recordings, from the 1920s, give a fairer idea of the choir's sound: strong and impressive, and well suited to the vastness of the Cathedral. Favourable comment continued, and in 1923 Gustav Holst wrote 'Nowadays every music-lover who is in London in Holy Week hopes to attend some, at least, of the musical services at Westminster Cathedral'.[6]

Not everyone, however, was in favour of what Terry was doing. Dissonant voices in the Catholic press disagreed with his interpretation of the papal document on sacred music; some wondered what had happened to the congregation's involvement, others believed that Terry was reversing the order of priority laid down by the Pope in putting so much stress on sixteenth-century polyphonic music at the expense of plainsong. More important from Terry's point of view were those who complained of the cost of it all; some of these found it useful to use the arguments for the priority of plainsong in what was basically a campaign to reduce the bills.

From the outset it was clear that it would be expensive to realize Cardinal Vaughan's plans for music in the Cathedral. Not only were eighteen priests employed as choir clergy, but a choir school had to be run and full-time men singers employed, if a balanced choir was to perform daily. This was in the context of a continual shortage of funds to cover the ordinary running costs of the Cathedral and frequent appeals to benefactors to subscribe towards completion of its fabric and ornamentation. Neither Cardinal Vaughan nor Cardinal Bourne wanted the Cathedral to be a burden which would interfere with the extension of the day-to-day work of the diocese, and both adopted the principle of not going ahead with any development of the Cathedral unless the money was already to hand.

It was reckoned that each of the boys in the Choir School cost £40 a year and that only about a third could afford to pay their own fees. The 'singing men', as they were referred to, were first engaged on contracts in 1903; there were nine of them, and the annual cost in wages was almost £800. By 1905 their number had risen to fifteen and the wages bill to £1,250; the total cost of the choir (including Terry's salary of £350) was estimated at over £1,975. Terry disputed the figure and argued that the true costs were £1,450, the sum which he had negotiated with Cardinal Vaughan just before the latter's death. Even if true, however, that sum was too high to be found every year. Vaughan had set up an endowment fund which was to bring in £1,000 a year; as early as November 1905, Bourne was appealing for extra donations 'to keep us going until the end of May', and a benefactor promised to try to raise £500 a year to keep the choir at its full strength. He failed, however, and it appears from the correspondence that funding the choir was not a particularly popular cause. Bourne hoped to raise sufficient funds by letting the vacant land beside the Cathedral on a long-term lease, but this plan also failed.[7]

Two ways to economize were suggested. One was to reduce the number of the men in the choir considerably, the other was to restrict the use of the full choir to Sundays and festivals so that the men would not have to be employed on a full-time basis. The first suggestion had the drawback that a greatly reduced choir would not have been able to sing the polyphonic music. The second, which was pushed more energetically, would have changed the whole character of the daily performance of the Divine Office. It rested on the proposal that the weekday services should be moved to a side chapel (probably the Lady Chapel) except on major festivals, and that the singing should be almost entirely in plainsong and done by the boys of the choir and the clergy. The proposers of this radical alteration argued that it would both add to the solemnity of the services which were carried out at the high altar, and be more in keeping with the Pope's pronouncements about the priority to be given to plainsong. In the end, savings were made by reducing the number of men singers, to nine in 1906 and to only six in 1912. The war inevitably reduced the number further, so that in 1918 there were only four men singers employed full-time. The daily services were not, however, relegated to a side chapel.

There was another problem that affected the daily performance which may be mentioned here. It concerned the clergy. As has been seen, the original idea was for a team of eighteen Cathedral Chaplains; these were to alternate weekly in two groups of nine to sing the Office and attend the daily High Mass. By the time the nine had provided a celebrant, a deacon, and a sub-deacon for the Mass, as well as a master of ceremonies, very few were left for the singing; holidays and sickness could on occasion reduce the numbers able to attend to nil. And, of course, not all were necessarily musical. One of them wrote in 1903 that there were currently four of their number who, no matter how often they practised, would never sing correctly or well.[8]

There was, of course, another group who could sing – the congregation at the services. One of the purposes of the Pope's musical reforms was to get the people to participate and to cease being merely listeners. Terry was very strongly in favour of congregational singing and felt that for many churches this would be far better than trying to get a choir together which would never be able to perform well. The congregation's technical ability was not important, nor even the quality of what they were singing; as he said, 'One's critical faculty refuses to exercise itself in the presence of so mighty a thing as a corporate outburst of praise'. He was sure that plainsong was ideal for congregational performance, and saw no reason why both the Proper and the Ordinary of the Mass should not be sung regularly by the people. It was to help to develop this approach that he wrote his various books and manuals to help and encourage Catholic choirmasters and teachers. The war, he felt, was teaching people that they could do very well without the services of their choirs as these were denuded of men and ceased to perform, and even in the Cathedral the 'heartiness of the singing was inspiring' on the occasions when the choir was dispensed with and the people sang.[9]

Given all of this, might he not have done more at the Cathedral to encourage the congregations to sing? There were those who believed that he should have spent more time on teaching the people plainsong, in line with the Pope's wishes, instead of concentrating so much on the choir. He did at one stage hold a series of regular practices for the people, for half an hour after Tuesday Benediction; no clear indication is given of what music was gone through on these occasions, but the comment that three new tunes were learnt at each session indicates that it was hymns for Benediction that were being taught. Perhaps he did not see it as part of his task as Master of Music to teach the people as well as the choir; perhaps there was not enough time; perhaps the nature of the building and changing make-up of the congregations themselves did not foster the cohesiveness found in a normal parish church. Was there too great a gap developing between the 'official' liturgy of the Cathedral and the 'ordinary' services of Mass and Benediction provided for the people?

It is interesting in this context that Terry's last public statements about the music at the Cathedral, made in the late 1930s long after he had retired from his post there, concerned the issue of the use of plainsong and supported the idea that it was the ideal form of music to encourage participation. He claimed that critics argued that it was not possible to get an ordinary congregation to sing without the 'support' of the organ, and that the music itself, being plain and without harmony, would be all the better for being 'brightened up' by the use of the organ. According to Terry, both arguments had been proved wrong by what had happened at the annual Mass for Peace in 1936: the *Credo* had been sung in plainsong by a miscellaneous congregation without any support and the effect had been 'thrilling'; at the same event, however, the organ had accompanied the choir in the singing of the other parts of the Mass in plainsong with the unfortunate effect of making it rigid as opposed to the 'free, fluent and unfettered' singing of the congregation.[10]

Terry frequently felt frustrated and let down by the constant battles which he had to fight with the authorities; he found the detail of paperwork irksome and was not good at it. He was bitter about the reduction in the size of his choir, and put it down to a failure to stick to Vaughan's ideals. His case would have been stronger, however, if he had not given so much ground for complaint himself. Apparently he would sometimes take off without leave for weeks at a time, leaving the boys to his assistant while he was away on a trawler tracking down sea shanties, or away at music festivals judging competitions. Cardinal Bourne had to write to him in 1911 because of the 'criticisms which reach me from every side' and insist on his attendance to his duties to train the boys and the men in person, not to cancel practice sessions, not to dismiss men from the choir without proper procedures, and so on. The most vocal of the critics felt that Terry had to be protected from himself because he took on far too many engagements outside his work at the Cathedral. The Cardinal put him firmly under the jurisdiction of the Administrator of the Cathedral, and the boys under the control at all times, even when they were in the Cathedral itself, of the Rector of the Choir School. This solved the immediate problems, but the tensions continued and when he finally resigned his post in 1924 Terry and a number of his friends felt that he had been badly treated and had not been given due recognition for all he had achieved. In a letter to *The Morning Post* he spoke of the pride he felt, but also of the 'sense of the deepest gratitude to those loyal souls who through good and bad report helped me to carry out as far as was humanly possible the great ideals of the great founder of the Cathedral, my ever revered master, Herbert Cardinal Vaughan'.[11]

In the end, what was his legacy? After reading so much about his revival of sixteenth-century English music one is perhaps tempted to think that there was a danger of the Cathedral's becoming a gigantic musical workshop. While it would never have become a musical museum, given his living interest in the connection between the music and the liturgy, there was occasionally an antiquarian air about the place, especially in the early war years when Terry was delving even further back, into pre-sixteenth-century music, some of which at least was of greater historical than musical interest. As has been said, he hated the very idea of musical élitism and of purely academic musicianship, but how many appreciated as he did the intimate link between the music of these early composers and the Catholic liturgy? Was there a contradiction between his espousal of such music and the stress on having the congregation involved which had been part of Vaughan's and Bentley's motivation in deciding on a style for the building? Perhaps he might have done more to promote congregational singing and participation, but what he did leave to those who followed him was a belief that only the best was good enough for the choral music in the Cathedral, and a standard that very few others could hope to attain either in the level of performance or in the link between that performance and the liturgy.

There was considerable concern over the question of a successor to Terry. Vaughan Williams, one of the few modern composers whose work Terry admired, expressed it very clearly in a letter to *The Times*. He urged the Cathedral authorities to show that a great ideal, once conceived, could be maintained and made permanent. That would require, he went on, the appointment of a musical director with skill and knowledge, and also with the authority and personality to carry things through in the face of possible opposition. He ended his letter 'All those who value dignity and nobility in the services of the Church (whatever their definition of the Church may be) must look anxiously to the lead which Westminster Cathedral is about to give'.[12] We do not know whether he was pleased or disappointed with the outcome. The new arrangements made by the Cardinal did ensure in one sense the maintenance of much of Terry's work, and even its permanence; the Holy Week music of, say, 1927 and 1928 bears a close resemblance to that of 1910 and 1911, but it appears to have been in some respects a routine repetition, lacking life and energy. Perhaps this is just to say that his successor was not as great a choir master or musician as Terry had been; perhaps, too, as a priest he was more under the control of the authorities and more hedged about by financial and other restrictions.

What the Cardinal did was to take the opportunity to make a complete rearrangement of the music at the Cathedral. He did not look for a lay person to replace Terry but appointed two priests instead: Fr Russell was to be Master of Music and Fr Lancelot Long was to be Choir Master. Both had worked with Terry   Russell was an organist and had on occasion acted as his assistant and Long had been one of the very first group of choirboys. Long had been ordained in 1914 – the first, it was hoped, of what would be a number of vocations from among the choirboys.[13] We can only guess at the Cardinal's motives in dividing the job in this way; it might well have been to prevent a single individual's becoming too dictatorial. The choice of priests instead of laymen was doubtless to save money in salaries and to make sure that overall control would rest more firmly in the Administrator's hands. A layman, Mr Hyde, was appointed to be full-time teacher of the members of the choir and also to be assistant organist.

Changes were also made in the make-up and duties of the choir. It was settled that the number of men should be six on weekdays and nine on Sundays; all were to be engaged subject to a month's notice and without formal written contracts. Much stricter regulations were laid down about attendance, the use of deputies, holidays and fines for absence. They were required to be in attendance daily at all services and at the regular practice sessions; for additional afternoon practices they would be paid another five shillings. There was a list of additional services for which they would also be paid extra; this included, interestingly enough, Christmas Eve Matins and Midnight Mass (ten shillings each), the *Tenebrae* services in Holy Week (also ten shillings) and the singing of the *Te Deum* on New Year's Eve (five shillings). It was also decided that all the men engaged in future should be Catholics – in the early days a majority of the men had been non-Catholics.[14]

The changes were effective in bringing stability throughout the 1920s and 1930s. There was little or no change in the style of music performed, and the balance between plainsong and polyphony was much as it had been in Terry's day. In 1927 Fr Long could write that the general scheme of Holy Week music at the Cathedral had by then become traditional, with the only variety coming from 'the names of pieces and composers'; the honours of the week were shared by the English and Italian schools of the fifteenth and sixteenth centuries. In the following year, however, he introduced a minor change: Masses by the English School were not used during Holy Week because, as Fr Long explained, they had been used far more during the year. As a result, 'the novelty of the Tudor school has now disappeared. Taverner, Shepherd, Ludforde, Fairfax are now familiar names to all who regularly attend the Cathedral.' He went on: 'What strange and diverse creatures mingle together in the common cause of music! Palestrina and his admirer Victoria; his pupil Anerio and Nanini the Roman; Di Lassus the Belgian; Handl the German; Philips and Dering the (English) exiles; Johnson the Scotsman; and Goudimel the Frenchman. In the English school, Tallis and Byrd, loyal to the Old Faith; Tye and Taverner, strong for the new.'[15]

Soon the Choir Master was defending himself against those whom he dismissed as superficial critics and disgruntled cranks. In an article in the *Cathedral Chronicle* in 1929 he spoke of the 'devout lady who wants Rossini's *Stabat Mater* on Good Friday and who refuses to be comforted by the Reproaches of Palestrina' and the 'extreme devotee of plainsong, who will have nothing but plainsong – and very plain at that – on Easter Day itself'. What is interesting about the article is its attack on plainsong. Long argued that it was fortunate that no law of the Church bound choirs to sing only the plainsong, 'since much of the chant is poor art . . . the Cathedral congregation should be thankful that it is spared the worst . . . the fanatic may rage, but anger will not turn bad chant into good music'. It was dangerous, he went on, to think that the 'official' music of the Church was always inspired and inspiring.

These were strange sentiments for the Choir Master to be putting into print in the official journal of the Cathedral in March 1929. Only a few months before, in December 1928, the Pope, Pius XI, had issued an Apostolic Constitution on Church Music, to mark the twenty-fifth anniversary of Pius X's *Motu Proprio*. The new Constitution underlined the main points of the previous statement, and again gave pride of place to plainsong, leaving no doubt that this was to be the preferred music of the Church's liturgy; polyphonic music kept second place because of its relationship to chant. Perhaps Long had not seen the full text of the papal Constitution when he had written his March article. In May he wrote again, explaining at some length the main points of the papal statement. What the Pope had written was not, he argued, a question of aesthetic taste but an authoritative statement of what was the best style for liturgical music, and the statement demanded obedience. What was needed according to the Pope was a revival of plainsong, and Long supported fully the plea that this must start in the seminaries, so that the clergy could then instruct the people in this sacred music, for the Pope made it clear that the congregation was to take part in the chant. In addition, Long pointed out that the Constitution laid down that those in charge of the music in basilicas and cathedrals were to see that these instructions were carried out properly. He could still say that even 'the most rampant partisans of the chant' had to admit that some of it was 'utterly worthless'; it was the style of the chant that the Popes were insisting on, not particular compositions. Those who loved the sacred liturgy would, he was sure, be grateful for the papal directives, for 'in Sacred as in Secular Music we are at the mercy of cranks and faddists; now these gentlemen must either learn more or talk less'. The article has the air of someone trying to justify a pattern of musical provision which was less than perfect according to a strict interpretation of papal statements, while at the same time supporting publicly all that the Popes had said.[16]

Clearly, Long felt that he had the mixture of the different types of music about right. While it was mainly a question of getting the right balance between plainsong and polyphony, there was also a third ingredient, and that was modern music by contemporary composers. From the start some people had hoped that, once the Cathedral had established itself as a centre of excellence for church music, new composers would feel moved to write for it and the Cathedral musicians in their turn would encourage them and welcome the opportunity to perform such works. Terry had hoped for the emergence of a new school of English church music. In 1919 he wrote 'hardly less important than the revival of old English music is the fact that the Cathedral services are creating a new school of church music by living English composers, writing in modern idiom, but in the spirit of the old masters and with the same restraint'. During the war Masses and motets by Holst, Charles Wood, (Fr) Antony Pollen, Howells, Thorogood and Bax were performed. Terry regarded Vaughan Williams's Mass in G minor as the best of all the new works, for it signified for him the break which had taken place between concert performances and acts of worship – something which Terry believed could not have happened even fifteen years before. He described these works (not all by Catholic composers) as the 'adorned liturgy' and the fulfilment of Pius X's *Motu Proprio* which had encouraged, if a little cautiously, the use of modern compositions.[17]

It is not surprising that by the late 1930s there were some people who believed that the music at the Cathedral had become fossilized and that a change of director would be of benefit. There were also those who still saw no need for a professional choir and wanted to see the whole system simplified, with the boys providing all the singing during the week and the congregation singing plainsong Masses on Sundays – this would avoid the costs of having the men singers, although these might still be used on certain days to add solemnity. The appointment of Archbishop Hinsley to succeed Cardinal Bourne in 1935 was seen by both groups as the occasion to push their views.

It was generally acknowledged that Fr Long had done a very competent job both as Choir Master and as headmaster of the Choir School. But the new Archbishop was urged to appoint a layman to be Master of Music, and to separate this post from the headship of the Choir School, which should be in the hands of a priest – 'and the less such a priest knows about music the better', said one of the Archbishop's advisors on the subject! The issue, however, could not be settled purely on musical grounds; as ever, there were financial implications. A priest who was one of the Cathedral chaplains cost very little – his keep and an annual stipend of only £60. It was estimated that to appoint a well-qualified lay person of sufficient standing would entail paying a salary of at least £500. As one outspoken critic put it, it was no use expecting people to do the work of geniuses on 'half the pay of a dustman'; if the work were done by a '£60 a year man' one could only expect music that most parish priests would refuse to tolerate in their churches.[18]

This was both unfair to Fr Long and unrealistic in its demands: the Cardinal could not make an appointment that would cost so much. As we will see in a later chapter, Hinsley had his own reasons for keeping expenditure on the Cathedral as low as possible and so no changes were made. Fr Long remained in effective charge until 1939 – he was described as 'Assistant' Master of Music and headmaster of the Choir School, with Fr Russell still Master of Music – when he was replaced by Fr William Stacey Bainbridge. Bainbridge in turn was replaced as Master of Music by a layman – William Hyde, one of Terry's 'singing men' who had been appointed in 1924 as assistant organist and teacher of the choir. So the Terry tradition continued, and the repertoire of the choir remained substantially as he had laid it down.[19]

Something should be said here about the Choir School itself. It had not been part of Cardinal Vaughan's original plans, but when his scheme for a monastic choir fell through he had to devise a way of providing a mixed choir of men's and boys' voices. He announced the foundation of a Choir School in 1901 and in the October of that year it opened with thirteen boys, whom the Cardinal welcomed as 'the foundations of the Cathedral'! They were housed in Archbishop's House and used one of the sacristies as their classroom and the Cathedral Hall as their playroom. Later they moved to a house in St George's Road, Pimlico. The first Rector of the School was the Rev. Dr Francis Aveling, a noted academic and Reader in Psychology at King's College, University of London. His staff consisted of two assistant masters (who were also priests) and a matron; as well as singing the boys were to learn English, Latin, French and Mathematics. Vaughan set up an endowment for seventeen scholars and eight exhibitioners; the fees were set at 50 guineas a year, remitted in full for the scholars, while the exhibitioners paid 20 guineas. The school acquired its own building in 1905 which provided boarding accommodation for 25 boys.[20]

By setting up a separate endowment for the school Vaughan hoped that it would not have to call on either the Cathedral or general diocesan funds. Unfortunately, the funds were invested in securities which were lost at the time of the Russian Revolution in 1917, and since then the school has been dependent on the parents' paying fees and on a subsidy from the diocese (not from the Cathedral funds).[21] Various attempts were made over the years to get enough money together to recreate the endowment but without success; as we will see in a subsequent chapter, the increasingly heavy subsidy which the school required brought about a crisis in the 1970s which threatened to close it altogether.

In the meanwhile, the school did a satisfactory job of providing boys for the choir, and this was its principal function. It appears that the general educational standards were not as high as they might have been – a headmaster in the 1960s was glad to be able to report that the days were gone when it could be said 'every year some of the boys sat for the School Certificate; none of them ever passed, of course'. A major change occurred in 1955 when the school underwent a general inspection by Her Majesty's Inspectors. They insisted that if the school were to continue to be recognized as 'efficient' there would have be a wholesale reorganization and, in particular, the employment of qualified teaching staff and a reduction in the hours which the boys spent in the Cathedral or in music practice. As the diocese could not dedicate four qualified priests just to one school, and could not afford to employ a lay staff for the purpose, the work was handed over to the Sisters of the Holy Cross. They helped to raise the academic standards and the school developed a reputation for its successes in the Common Entrance Examinations. The Sisters continued at the school until a shortage of vocations forced them to withdraw in 1972.[22]

In the early days the regime for the boys was spartan and authoritarian – in many ways the school seems to have been run on lines similar to the junior seminaries of the day, and, indeed, it was hoped that it would be a fruitful source of vocations to the priesthood. Terry was a hard taskmaster whom the boys found intimidating but his reputation was such that they were involved in a range of activities outside their official duties – in contrast to the restrictive pattern which developed later. For example, they sang at charity concerts around London, supplied the treble voices for performances of the Western Madrigal Society of London, and visited the HMV recording studios at Hayes to make a large number of recordings, not all of sacred music by any means. It must have been a unique and rewarding musical experience, perhaps compensating to some extent for the loss of ordinary schooling that it undoubtedly involved.[23] The school was still operating in much the same way down to the outbreak of the war in 1939. At first the boys were moved out of London to a country house near Uckfield, in Sussex, but then the school was closed altogether and the music in the Cathedral was performed by a reduced body of professional men singers.

The Choir School was reopened in the spring of 1946, and the task of forming a new choir for the Cathedral fell at first to Hyde. There were some problems in getting enough boys to attend the school, since the number of Catholic parents willing to pay fees for that particular type of education was still small; almost every applicant had to be accepted, regardless of the quality of his voice. Another problem lay in getting men for the choir: the pay was poor, and the financial constraints meant that there were never enough male singers to balance the boys. But Hyde, who had done the difficult job of keeping the music alive during the war years successfully, managed to train the new boys and to re-create the choir. In January 1947, it was taken over by the new Master of Music, George Malcolm.[24] Malcolm was a musician of outstanding ability. Born in 1917 and educated at the Royal College of Music and Balliol, Oxford, he was a pianist and conductor, and later made a considerable name as a harpsichordist and became Associate Conductor of the BBC Scottish Orchestra, being awarded a CBE in 1965. He was Master of Music at the Cathedral from 1947 to 1959 and set the highest of standards for the choir.

To begin with he kept William Hyde on as his assistant and was happy with the work that he had done as caretaker choirmaster with one exception, and that was the tone of the boys' singing. He described the sound which had been developed from Terry's days onwards as a 'hooty, Anglican' sound, which he wished to replace with something more like that produced by the successful Jesuit choirmasters at their Wimbledon and Farm Street parish churches. He believed that the Anglican cathedral sound was too artificial and ruined the pronunciation of the language, whether English or Latin – he later caricatured it as making 'Amen' sound like 'Oomoon' – the boys' voices were trained to become 'tuneful little instruments which will echo back sweetly from the Gothic vaulting and never crack a stained-glass window'. He admitted that their sound was 'pure', but it was the purity of an emasculated angel on a Christmas card. His aim was to get the boys singing instead of hooting; this was easier to achieve because of the break which had occurred during the war. When critics and other choirmasters heard his new sound there was some consternation: it was, they claimed, Continental and un-English, and too strong to be natural for boys' voices. Malcolm, on the other hand, said that what he was doing was using the sound normally produced by boys – at one stage he referred to singing as 'a controlled form of shouting'! In the end his choir produced a sound which was clear and strong, suited to the size of the Cathedral, and which had more character than much of the rather bland, emotionless sound produced by Cathedral choirs up to then. Such was his and the choir's later reputation that others began to adopt the technique or at least to modify the traditional English choral sound.[25]

Another of Malcolm's aims was to increase the number of men in the choir. This had dropped to three when he took over, and although he was able to recruit more, he believed that there were never enough to balance the boys properly. The men were, he claimed, miserably paid, and he fought a running battle to have their wages increased.

The choir's regular schedule imposed heavy demands. There were fifteen services each week (seven High Masses, seven sung Vespers, and sung Compline on Sundays); if one adds the additional heavy load at Easter and Christmas, and other special services, one can understand how there was no time for anything in the way of concerts or recording. Indeed, the Cathedral Administrators made it very clear that they had not the slightest interest in the choir's performing apart from its regular duties. Mgr Collingwood imposed a very restrictive regime, and even though Malcolm found his successor, Gordon Wheeler, to be a 'breath of fresh air' in comparison, the choir was still not given any encouragement to expand its activities. In 1951, for example, when it was felt that the choir should do something as part of the Festival of Britain, a 'Festival Week of Music' was put on. This consisted of the normal daily services, sung to what was described as 'a specially chosen programme of music': plainsong, sixteenth-century polyphony (six English composers), some eighteenth-century pieces (including a Mozart motet) and a few moderns – Terry, Elgar, Hyde and Malcolm himself. One wonders whether regular attenders would have noticed very much 'special' about the week. There were occasional broadcasts: in 1955, for example, a 'Preparation for Christmas' service was broadcast consisting of choral pieces by Palestrina, Malcolm and Sweelinck, scriptual readings and short talks by Wheeler.[26]

The general ban on outside activities was not just due to a fear that other activities might have eaten into the time needed to practise and perform its main role. Wheeler had what he himself described as 'an absolute phobia' about the Cathedral's being used for concerts, even of sacred music, and in this he was fully supported by both Cardinal Griffin and Cardinal Godfrey. The former was in total agreement with his Administrator, for example, when he refused permission for a performance of Elgar's *Dream of Gerontius* to be held in the Cathedral, even though the first London performance of the work had been given in the Cathedral in 1903; Wheeler explained that the difference was that the building had not then been consecrated. An earlier request to use the Cathedral had been refused even though Sir John Barbirolli had written to support it. An exception was made for organ recitals which had become something of a tradition and were usually given on a weekday evening. (The tradition continues with the Sunday afternoon recitals before Benediction.) It is not clear why these were not regarded as 'concerts' and so forbidden. Part of the reason may have been that they caused no interruption in the daily liturgy for practices to be held, for this was one of the objections put forward by Wheeler and others to the putting on of concerts. Perhaps, too, they smacked less of performances, though organists of international renown were engaged to give them.[27]

The choir did make two recordings during Malcolm's time: one was of Victoria's *Tenebrae* music, the other of Benjamin Britten's *Missa Brevis* which he had written especially for the boys' choir. The first had to be made during the holidays, as no time was allowed for it during term time; the second was unintentional and came about as follows. At Christmas the choir used to sing carols in the Cathedral every day between Christmas and the Epiphany, and in 1958 they sang Britten's 'Ceremony of Carols' with the composer present. He was so moved that he asked Malcolm if he could write something for the choir, and Malcolm said that the best thing would be a Mass for the boys' voices in two or three parts with organ accompaniment. Britten agreed, but had not produced anything by the time Malcolm had decided to resign in July 1959. They met accidentally, and on hearing the news of Malcolm's impending retirement Britten finished the Mass in two weeks and it was performed in the Cathedral. The BBC had got to know of the occasion and recorded the performance live without any practice or testing. Britten was so pleased that he persuaded a record company to buy the tapes from the BBC and to issue them commercially as a record. It should not be thought, however, that the Masters of Music or the choir felt particularly constrained by the prevailing attitude of the Administrators with regard to concerts and outside engagements. Their regular duties kept them very busy, and concerts and recordings had not become the fund-raising industry that has developed since then.[28]

There appear to have been few links between the Master of Music and the clergy choir although the latter 'shared' the singing with the lay choir. There was a period of six months or so when Malcolm was asked to organize practices for the chaplains who formed the clergy choir, but there was little enthusiasm for them; he lamented the fact that an aptitude for sacred music was not among the criteria used in the appointment of the chaplains. Nor was anything done to encourage the congregation at the services to participate apart from getting them to sing the *Gloria* and *Credo* in plainsong at the Sunday High Mass.

By the time Malcolm decided to retire from the post of Master of Music (in order to develop his career as a concert performer), changes in the Church's liturgy had begun to be introduced – the Dialogue Mass, and the revised

Easter ceremonies, for example. The full impact of these and subsequent changes on the liturgical life of the Cathedral will be dealt with in a later chapter. It is sufficient to note here that they involved major alterations to what had been the musical highlight of the year from Terry's time onwards: the office of *Tenebrae* on Wednesday, Maundy Thursday and Good Friday had been the occasion of a *tour de force* of polyphonic music, and the programme of music sung in Holy Week 1948, for example, included many of the same compositions that Terry would have used (though with a very marked reduction in the use of sixteenth-century English composers). The new rite for Holy Week did away with the office of *Tenebrae* altogether. Some years later it was decided that too much of the Cathedral's musical tradition had been lost because of this change, and a special para-liturgical service was arranged for the evening of the Wednesday in Holy Week. In this a variation of the old *Tenebrae* service was introduced which allowed for the singing of much of the old Holy Week music.[29] At the time there was understandable regret at the reduction in a fine musical tradition, but the changes did not immediately affect the heart of the choir's work, which continued to be the servicing of the daily capitular liturgy.

Malcolm had rebuilt and improved the choir to make it one of the outstanding cathedral choirs in the country. His achievement was one of the factors which contributed to the reputation of the 1950s as the 'great days' of the Cathedral, when the Vaughan 'vision' came closest to being realized. Fine music enhanced the meticulous daily performance of the Divine Office, while at the same time the pastoral side of the Cathedral's mission was being extended. This period will be looked at more fully in a later chapter. Before that, it is necessary to turn to another area and to see what was being done to complete Bentley's unfinished masterpiece.

NOTES

1   *Motu Proprio*: English translation in R. Terry, *Catholic Church Music* (1907).
2   See the Benedictines of Stanbrook, *In a Great Tradition* (1956).
3   E. Oldmeadow, *Francis Cardinal Bourne* (2 vols, 194?), II, p. 338.
4   H. Andrews, *Westminster Retrospect: A Memoir of Sir Richard Terry* (Oxford, 1948) – a very knowledgable, though somewhat uncritical, study. See also T. Day, *A Discography of Tudor Church Music* (1989), pp. 17ff.
5   *Westminster Cathedral Chronicle* (1910 and 1921).
6   See Day for the early phase and Terry's achievement, and p. 18 for Holst. He also gives details of the re-issues of the early recordings by the choir.
7   AAW, Bo 5/47a, for the letters and suggestions for economies.
8   Ibid.

9   *Chronicle* (1910, and 1918 for series of articles by Terry).
10 *The Tablet* (18 April 1936 and 3 April 1937).
11 See Andrews; and Cardinal's letters in AAW, Bo 1/23.
12 Vaughan Williams to *The Times*, cutting in AAW, Bo 1/23.
13 Long wrote an account of his early choir days in 1925; reprinted *Chronicle* (May 1973), pp. 6–9.
14 AAW, Bo 1/23.
15 *Chronicle* (1926–29), 'Handl the German' is the sixteenth-century Jakob Handl.
16 Ibid. (February–May 1929) for Pius XI's Constitution, and Long's articles.
17 Ibid. (1919).
18 AAW, Hi 2/42.
19 *Catholic Directories* for relevant years.
20 W. de l'Hopital, *Westminster Cathedral and Its Architect* (1919), I, p. 302; some accounts give St George's Road, others Cambridge Street; Long gives 1906 as the date.
21 *Chronicle* (1955).
22 Ibid. and see August 1968 and November 1972.
23 B. Gilsenen, *Chronicle* (December 1968), and B. Langley, *Bulletin* (July/August 1993).
24 Author's interview with George Malcolm (August 1993), and *Bulletin* (February 1993).
25 Author's interview; BBC interview with James O'Donnell, (19 August 1992); Day, p. 33.
26 *Chronicle* (1951 and 1955).
27 AAW, Go 2/22 (1956–57) and *Chronicle*.
28 Author's interview with George Malcolm.
29 *Chronicle* (February 1972).

Chapter 5

Marble and mosaic: decorating the Cathedral

HAD BENTLEY LIVED LONGER, he would have involved himself in every aspect of the Cathedral's decoration and furnishings. He would have produced drawings for every detail, from electric chandeliers to chalices, from confessionals to the choice of marbles, and all would have witnessed to his meticulous craftsmanship and his vision of the building as a single whole. In areas in which he was not himself expert he would have supervised the work of others with painstaking attention. He did leave drawings and sketches, some only partly finished, for much of the work that remained to be done, and because of this, and because he had told a number of people of his ideas and schemes, some people felt that the Cathedral could be completed in accordance with his wishes in almost every detail. When he spoke at Bentley's funeral, Cardinal Vaughan said that it would be necessary for the 'perfection of the work' to retain Bentley's mind as a guide. Everyone knew, he went on, what had happened to St Peter's and other buildings when 'the plan and genius of the original architecture' were not followed. 'Let us', he concluded, 'maintain the main idea and the unity of Bentley's work to the end.'[1]

Arrangements were made to ensure the desired continuity: a firm named John F. Bentley, Son and Marshall was set up. John Marshall had been Bentley's chief assistant for some years, and became the new chief architect for the Cathedral, while Bentley's son, Osmond, joined the firm as soon as his architectural training had been completed. But, of course, absolute faithfulness to Bentley's ideas was not possible. In the first place, he had not left drawings for everything, and it was left to later artists and designers to interpret and carry out what they thought would be in keeping with his ideas. And even before his architect's death Vaughan had not always carried out his wishes – we have seen this with regard to the pulpit, the throne, and most of all, the flooring of the nave of the Cathedral. As late as the 1960s debates were still taking place about whether plans for particular schemes of decoration (in, for example, the baptistery) would have pleased Bentley or not. It is easy to imagine, therefore, how hot the critics became in the years immediately after his death when they thought his 'mind' was no longer being followed, and even more when his explicit designs were rejected; the most obvious example here is the choice of Eric Gill's Stations of the Cross, which will be examined later in this chapter.

If, as was likely even in Vaughan's time, it was going to take many years to complete the interior of the building, striving after complete faithfulness to Bentley's ideas was even less likely to be possible; was it even desirable? Bentley himself had refused to follow any one type or period of building; rather, he had borrowed and adapted and created, achieving in the end a marvellous and original unity. What succeeding generations had to do was to provide the best artistic work for its decoration and completion, according to the artistic principles of their own day. They had, as it were, to reinterpret the building, doing nothing that would obscure Bentley's original statement but seeking to increase its spiritual impact by drawing inspiration from their personal faith and the needs of the liturgy of their time, as Bentley himself had done. Vaughan had wanted a 'live' cathedral; such a building must surely reflect the ages through which it has lived.

Bentley had planned for the interior to be magnificently coloured, with dozens of different kinds of marble on the floor and walls, and great fields of mosaic covering the domes, arches and other spaces. Now, English Catholic religious art in the nineteenth century had been marked on the whole by what appears to us to have been a sentimental realism or naturalism in painting and sculpture. How would his fellow Catholics react to Bentley's new decorative schemes, reminiscent as they were of Continental churches of past ages and different artistic fashions? How readily would they adapt to the absence of shrines of freestanding statues and pictures, both alien to the general Byzantine spirit of the new building? Above all, how would they react to widespread mosaic and how would artists and designers interpret Bentley's intentions with regard to this medium?

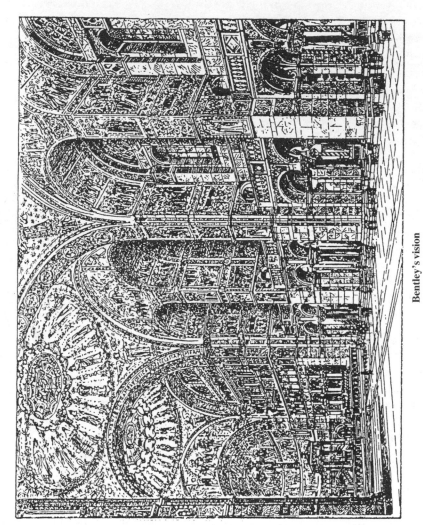

Bentley's vision

This early drawing by an unknown artist shows what Bentley had in mind for the
decoration of the interior

English artists were taking an increasingly active interest in mosaic work towards the end of the nineteenth century; there were firms which specialized in the medium, and a successful painter like Sir William Richmond was happy to take on a commission for extensive mosaic work for St Paul's in London. There was considerable debate in learned bodies such as the Royal Institute of British Architects about the best methods to use, and a growing literature on the mosaics to be found in early Christian buildings. There had never been, of course, a strong English native tradition in the medium, and so there could not be the almost instinctive understanding of its potential and limitations such as could be found elsewhere in Europe, especially in Italy. We have seen that Bentley had gone there for inspiration, especially to Ravenna and Venice. Soon after he had become Archbishop, Cardinal Bourne had gone to Monreale and Palermo in Sicily to study the mosaics there.[2] But even in the home of early Christian architecture, Ravenna, the lessons to be learned were not straightforward. The same building could contain different styles side by side: some designs were naturalistic, with faces that were portraits, figures that were flexible and backgrounds that were 'real' with trees, rocks and animals; others were rigid and formal, with blue or gold backgrounds and no attempt to portray a landscape. Both styles were rich in Christian symbolism.[3] Which should be the model for the new Cathedral? The learned debates already referred to showed an almost total lack of agreement among the experts as to style, type of material and methods of fixing to be used in modern mosaic work. Whatever Bourne and Marshall chose to do there would be controversy.

Bentley spoke of the Cathedral as a 'veneered' building: for him the main purpose of the mosaic would be decorative. This may seem obvious, but not everyone who put forward schemes for the work saw it in this way; some wanted the decoration to be also instructive, along the lines, perhaps, of the old medieval wall-paintings; others wanted it to celebrate England's Catholic heritage, with scenes mythical and historical from Glastonbury to Wiseman. Nor did they all appreciate the problems caused by the size of the building: what might be seen to advantage in a side chapel would be lost in the vastness of the main domes. Bentley was keen to plan the decoration of the whole with some overarching scheme based on the principal themes of Christian salvation, and believed that this should be done before any attempt was made to plan the side chapels. It was decided, however, to push ahead with two of the chapels first, mainly because donors had given sufficient money for them to be completed, but also because it was felt that the successful completion of the two would encourage other donors to come forward. One of these chapels was dedicated to the Holy Souls in Purgatory, the other to St Gregory and St Augustine, the apostles of England.

The artist chosen to design the mosaics for the Holy Souls Chapel was Christian Symons. When Bentley wrote to him about the commission he said that 'anything pictorial' had to be avoided; the design would have to be 'severe and very Greek' in character. It is clear, however, that he did not mean by this that the design would be abstract, for in a later letter he thought that Purgatory itself could be represented, with St Michael on one side leading souls out and St Raphael, as the angel of death, on the other side leading others in. Perhaps instead of 'pictorial' he might have written 'realistic' or 'naturalistic'. Again, in this letter, he stressed the need for a simple design in the Greek style. He involved himself in every aspect of the work, which was carried out by a Mr George Bridge and his team of female mosaicists working from a studio in Oxford Street. The finished chapel won general praise from critics at the time; it was unusual in that the barrel roof was given a background in silver, instead of the usual blue or gold, as being more suitable to the sombre nature of the chapel's dedication. Among the scenes depicted are Adam and the serpent, and the three boys in the fiery furnace, while the altarpiece shows Christ enthroned, with Mary and Joseph interceding for the Holy Souls. It has been claimed frequently that this chapel could be taken as a successful example of what Bentley had in mind as the ideal in mosaic decoration, since it was completed in his lifetime and under his supervision. There is evidence, however, that he was not happy with the work as it appeared when completed, and certainly Lethaby, one of his strongest supporters, felt that it was weak with a 'sentimental vulgarity'.[4]

Work on the decoration of a second chapel, that dedicated to St Gregory and St Augustine, was begun while the architect was still alive. The donors were Lord and Lady Brampton; the initial plan was that it should become a Brampton Chantry, with effigies of the donors, but this was not carried through. Lord Brampton insisted on choosing the designer and mosaicist himself, and so the commission was given to the firm of Clayton and Bell. Bentley was hardly involved. Clayton was a 'modernist' and believed that it was a mistake for artists to try to use styles from the past: he repudiated both Byzantine and Greek, and insisted on using the contemporary Italian method of fixing the mosaic – this used very regular pieces and fitted them together with hardly any joints showing and into as flat a surface as possible; critics thought that this produced a much duller surface than that produced by the older, more irregular methods. There was also a greater stress on realism in the pictures telling the story of St Gregory and the conversion of

England. A comparison of the two chapels illustrates very clearly the differences of opinion even among experts about the use of mosaic. It is also another example of the influence which a generous donor could exert against the wishes of the architect. One feels for the Cardinal, caught in a critical storm and, on occasion, subject to the patronizing scorn of the artistic establishment and contemporary aesthetes when he was honestly trying to carry out Bentley's ideas.[5] Bourne's biographer claims that many worshippers were deeply moved by the 'smouldering mystery' of the Holy Souls Chapel, while being far less inspired by the 'more pictorial and explicit decoration' of the other chapel. It seems to have been after this that Bourne decided to visit those places in Italy where the best examples of ancient mosaic work could be studied, so that he would be better able to judge future designs for himself. Now that the critical storm is long over the contrast between the two chapels, and the different results obtained using the same materials, can be taken as part of the Cathedral's overall interest.

Some work was also done in these early years on the decoration of the Lady Chapel. Considerable discussion had taken place about a decorative scheme for the whole chapel, but in the end only the reredos and the recesses in the apse were completed to designs by a well-known mosaicist, Robert Anning Bell, who had designed some of the mosaic panels in the Houses of Parliament. The altarpiece, which shows the Virgin and Child, was considered to be fully Byzantine at the time in that the artist had understood the limitations of the material and had not tried to produce a realistic 'picture'. On the other hand, the pieces of mosaic used were very even in size and shape, unlike the early, more rough-cut work, and the finished piece is, perhaps, a little flat and regular if one is using Ravenna as a model. But its clean lines are attractive and the whole is uncluttered, unlike some of the other mosaics which are overladen with detail. The piece was well received at the time, and in later years was held up as a successful example of mosaic work – especially during the controversies which unfortunately surrounded almost all the other decorative work done during Bourne's years.

The Cardinal chose Anning Bell again in 1916 to do the mosaic work on the tympanum over the main west door of the Cathedral. Because of its position this was obviously a very important commission, and Bourne had delayed taking a decision for ten years, although he had money in hand; he clearly found the whole issue of the mosaic decoration very perplexing and his natural caution added to the difficulty. Bentley had left the outline of a design which had been elaborated by Marshall some years later. This was followed in the main by Anning Bell, but there were some important differences in the finished work, the main one being the background, which was left white, apparently from a fear that the London climate and atmosphere would ruin anything in the traditional blue or gold. Although Bourne expressed his great disappointment with this work, and others criticized it for departing from Bentley's design and for its 'dead' white background, it won general approval from the critics. This was in contrast with the public row over the other major work completed about this time – the chapel of St Andrew and the Scottish Saints, opened to the public in 1915.[6]

Here again the Cardinal was put in a difficult position by the wishes of the most generous benefactor. The fourth Marquess of Bute had offered £10,000 to pay for the complete decoration of the Scottish chapel, on condition that he could choose the artist to design and carry out the work. Bourne agreed, and the commission was given to Mr R. W. S. Weir, a respected authority on Byzantine art, a former member of the British School at Athens and secretary of the Byzantine Research and Publication Fund. (His original name was Robert Weir Schultz; on the outbreak of war in 1914 he changed it to avoid the anti-German feeling of the day; he was a Scot by descent.) A large part of his work had been done for the third and fourth Marquesses of Bute, and it was not at all surprising that the latter, with his interest in Byzantine art, should have chosen him to decorate his chapel in the great Byzantine Cathedral. He was able to design the decoration of the whole chapel, including the altar, the marbles for the floor and lower walls and the mosaics; later, in 1924, he designed a confessional which was set into the outside wall of the chapel.

When the chapel was finally opened to the public, criticism was centred mainly on two aspects: the cold colours of the marbles, and the style of the mosaics. Of the first, an art critic in *The Times* wrote that it was 'positively freezing in its colourless coldness . . . colour-blindness could not have led to a more deplorable result'. Another thought that going into the chapel was like going into a bathroom and being 'up to the neck in cold water'! Weir's biographer suggests that working in the heart of English Catholicism brought out the cold dourness in the Scottish Presbyterian. With regard to the mosaics, what annoyed the critics most of all was the figure of St Andrew himself on the wall opposite to the altar, which was described as being 'void of dignity and expression'. On the other hand, they praised the roof which had been covered simply in a gold mosaic pattern, variously interpreted as representing clouds screening paradise, or fishscales symbolizing St Andrew's origins. Some critics also liked the way in which the four cities connected with the saint had been depicted in a very Byzantine manner, but others quibbled with the contrast between the 'colourless' marbles and the warmth of the mosaics. The Cardinal may have drawn some comfort from the fact that two professional journals, *The Builder* and *Building News*, praised the chapel, while a respected architect of the day, Mr C. Townsend, himself an expert on ancient mosaics, thought it was 'one of the most beautiful works of decoration ever done in England . . . with the full dignity of old Byzantine work'; the work in the chapel, he felt, was the only work so far done in the Cathedral which breathed the true spirit of Byzantine art. The overall result, he concluded, was full of 'impressiveness, richness and beauty'. Weir's biographer says that the chapel was the 'final and perfect expression of his interest in Byzantine art and of his adherence to the ideals of the Arts and Crafts movement'.[7]

A feature of the chapel which deserves special mention are the very fine stalls and kneelers. The kneelers were the work of Sidney Barnsley, the stalls of Ernest Gimson – it is unclear what part Weir played in the design, which has Orthodox overtones. Pevsner claims that the stalls, which he says are of ebony inlaid with ivory, are amongst Gimson's finest work, 'indeed amongst the best decorative woodwork of its date anywhere in Europe . . . slender upright forms and crisp dainty inlay'. There is a Cathedral tradition that the materials used were Scottish bog oak and antler horn; these would have been ideally suited to the decoration of the chapel, which used Scottish materials wherever possible. Gimson's biographer, Lethaby, however, is clear that the stalls were of brown ebony (which Gimson used frequently) and bone. Weir, Barnsley, Gimson and Lethaby had all worked closely together at various times and all of them had been strongly influenced by the Arts and Crafts movement.[8]

Another part of the furnishings which were being completed at this time were the Stations of the Cross. Here the choice of an artist seems to have been left to the architect, John Marshall. Again, there was both praise and condemnation at the time for Eric Gill's work, with subsequent writers seeing them as amongst the finest things in the Cathedral. Gill was surprised to be chosen: he was only beginning to make a name for himself, and had only just become a Catholic. In his autobiography he claimed that the reason for the choice was financial and not artistic: the architect told him that if he had not been willing to do the job at a price which no 'posh' artist would look at then he would not have been given the commission. He also claimed that the Cardinal was losing patience with Marshall over the delay, as the 'pious donors were getting restive'; if someone were not chosen quickly the Cardinal threatened to give the work to the first Catholic he met in the street. Gill felt that, even so, Bourne would not have agreed to the commission if he had seen a finished carving of any of the Stations – a sign, perhaps, that the Cardinal was not too pleased with the panels as they began to be erected in the Cathedral.[9]

Gill's views about the Cathedral in general were far from complimentary. He thought it 'as disagraceful a piece of sham stylistic building as any Pugin Gothic . . . The outside of the building is absurd. The inside will soon be equally so.' While he later admitted that Bentley's plans had been 'noble' and had created a 'great interior space', its ornament was 'dead' and the plan to cover it all in marble and mosaic 'ridiculous'. But he accepted the commission, and spent from 1914 to 1918 working on it. The individual Stations were erected as they were completed, sometimes individually, sometimes three or four at a time, and not necessarily in sequence. Gill's ideas and ability developed as the work progressed; at one stage he experimented with blues, reds and greens to add some colour to the Hoptonwood stone (not marble, as some writers said at the time), but he later removed them. In his autobiography he concluded: 'some of them are good, even if some of them are bad', and, he added, as no two people agreed which was which, nothing could be done about it![10]

Critical opinion was divided. Some of those who condemned the Stations did so in exaggerated language, talking about them as 'pseudo-primitive', 'strangely crude', 'an affront to the people and to God'; one writer spoke of the Cathedral's becoming the 'laughing stock of all artistic London' because the stations were 'ugly, queer and comic'! Others felt that the low-relief carving and plain stone were stylistically out of keeping with the rest of the building, although the original idea of using coloured *opus sectile* tiles would surely have been much worse from that point of view. When some critics claimed that Gill had deliberately chosen a Byzantine style, he replied that he might have done the carving in what could be called an 'archaic manner', but not deliberately to copy a particular style – he just could not carve in any other way. The figures have been well described as a compromise between the rigidity of genuine Byzantine forms and the movement to be found in Western art: the attitudes of the figures and their dress imply movement but do not portray it in any realistic way.[11]

The finished work must have looked very strange to a non-artistic Catholic worshipper of the time, so used to Stations of the Cross which were pictorial and emotional. *The Universe*, for example, was full of angry letters, and one writer urged the Cardinal to issue a statement that the Stations were only in place temporarily and that there was 'never any intention of leaving them as a permanent annoyance to Catholics and a blot on the Cathedral'. Because of the criticism, Gill felt he had to defend what he had done. He did not, he wrote in the *Cathedral Chronicle* under a pseudonym, see the Stations as 'works of art', but as part of the furnishing of the Cathedral; they were in place to lead people to prayer and devotion, and to promote the Church's ideas, not the artist's – that was why he had left aside his own ideas about costume, the faces of the figures and their emotions. In a very telling phrase, Gill said that the Stations should be as neutral as the beads on a rosary – the meditation and prayer had to come from the individual. Again, he said that he had omitted the crowd from the panels because we, the worshippers, were the crowd and had to supply the reactions and the emotions; the artist should not be asked to do this for us.[12]

It was this restraint that some writers praised at the time, finding in it a welcome break from what one of them called the 'gaudy and meaningless Italian symbols' which Gill's opponents would have put in their place. It was not the artist's fault, he continued, if 'generations of bad taste or complete lack of taste' had prevented Catholic chapels in England from being well decorated. Supporters of the Stations were in a minority at the time, but subsequent writers have come to see them as very fine. Pevsner praised them as one of the first works of religious art in England to abandon sentimental realism, while more recently they have been seen as evidence of Gill's ability to integrate wall monuments into the overall design of a building; the panels pick up the side lighting that the Cathedral provides as though they are part of the structure itself. Gill himself, as we have seen, did not think they were successful in every detail; nor was he very interested in how they might be judged as 'works of art': they were genuine stone carvings rather than copies of things done in stone. He understood the possibilities and the limitations of his material just as the best of the ancient mosaicists had theirs.[13]

Cardinal Bourne's final contribution to the decoration of the Cathedral was to choose the artist, Gilbert Pownall, to design and execute the mosaics for the key areas above the sanctuary and the choir. When the critics consistently attacked the artist's work he felt he had to write to defend his choice. The Cathedral was not, he wrote, a museum of art, but a house of prayer; nothing must hinder, and everything should assist, the 'piety of the ordinary faithful Catholic'. Nor should the Archbishop be regarded as a source of commissions for artists who then disregarded his preferences and ideas or even treated them with 'veiled disdain'. He had refused to have a committee of experts to advise him, for he would have been faced with 'clamant, loud-voiced, contradictory opinions'; he could only study the matter carefully, see all the ancient mosaic work himself and seek individual advice from the best sources in England and abroad. He continued to support Pownall and, to the dismay of the critics, praised the work he did in completing the Lady Chapel and the great tympanum over the altar. Nor did he please them when he had the large cross taken down from the sanctuary; he claimed that it had been an 'afterthought' and should be removed as it was too large and obstructed the view of the mosaics.[14]

The Cardinal had been doing what he thought best to follow Bentley's ideas, within the limits of the inevitable financial constraints and what he thought would suit the people who used the Cathedral. He had not acted quickly in choosing Pownall, and the latter's designs had been on public display for several months before they were accepted. He had come to the conclusion that only a Catholic artist should be employed, for only a Catholic could have the depth of understanding and feeling for the truths and traditions of the Catholic faith which would ensure their satisfactory artistic interpretation. In an attempt to cut down on the costs, and to ensure that the work of completing the rest of the mosaics could be carried out with some continuity of style and method, he had established a 'school of mosaicists' with their own workshop in the tower of the Cathedral. It must have been galling for him to read in the national press that the results of all his thought and effort were condemned as 'amateurish, clumsy, without mastery and without beauty', and that it was leading to the ruination of Bentley's great building.[15]

The principal critic was Edward Hutton, a Catholic writer on art and the holder of the British Academy Medal for Italian Studies. It was unfortunate that the *Cathedral Chronicle* had tried to defuse his criticism by attacking him personally, questioning his standing and suggesting that *The Daily Telegraph* had made up his credentials. When Bourne was succeeded by Cardinal Hinsley in March 1935, Hutton organized an appeal to stop the mosaic work that Pownall was still doing. It was signed by leading figures of the artistic establishment – the President of the Royal Academy, the Slade Professor of Art at Oxford, the Director of the Tate Gallery, the President of the Catholic Art Guild, Sir Giles Gilbert Scott, the Director of the National Gallery (Kenneth Clark), the Director of the Victoria and Albert Museum, members of the Royal Fine Arts Commission and others, including Eric Gill. The appeal expressed their 'disquietude' at the decorative work that had been carried out in recent years and called for the Archbishop to halt the damage being done to 'Bentley's great church, the mother church of England's Catholicism', which was one of London's 'most significant architectural achievements . . . a national monument'.[16]

The Cardinal agreed to stop Pownall's work. Shortly afterwards he set up a committee to advise him on everything artistic to do with the Cathedral, consisting of two clergymen and three lay experts. In the meantine, Pownall threatened legal action for breach of contract and was eventually given £2,000 by way of settlement. Hutton was later to design the fine floor in St Paul's chapel, drawing his inspiration from one of the famous chapels at Palermo in Sicily and producing a strong pattern of white Pentelic marble (the sort used in the Parthenon in Athens) inlaid with porphyry, red and green, and, incidentally, proving that his original criticism of Pownall's work was not just that of a self-styled expert. The floor was laid just before the outbreak of World War II.[17]

While Hinsley's action in stopping Pownall was taken at the time to be the result of external artistic pressure, it seems that he was happy to do so for quite different reasons. In a letter of December 1935, to Bishop Myers, his Auxiliary, he wrote that his main reason for discontinuing the work was that he believed he should not be spending money on 'unnecessary work' at a time when Catholic schools and other necessities called for every penny. As long as 'luxury' work continued it would be very difficult to argue that the poverty of the Catholic body justified asking for increased grants for the schools; the Church, he felt, was thought to be immensely wealthy. He decided that he would not allow any appeals for the decoration of the Cathedral, nor even encourage donations for that purpose. About the same time he wrote to an architect to praise his simple designs for Catholic churches: churches could be majestic in their simplicity, he wrote, and he found it unacceptable to build costly ones when 'the living stones, immortal souls, are perishing for want of opportunities to learn the faith'. In addition to these reasons, he had doubts about the 'school of mosaicists', especially given the circumstances of what was happening in Italy where the raw materials for the work came from.[18]

There was in this initial reaction a throwback to Manning's concerns and insistence that education for the poor was a greater priority than building the Cathedral in the first place. The provision of Catholic schools had dominated clerical thought and effort in England for seventy or eighty years, and dedication to that cause had become a test of orthodoxy. Bourne had been accused of neglecting the building of schools in the diocese in favour of spending money on the diocesan seminary, but Hinsley made it his cause, although he did not understand the intricacies of the system or all the problems involved – some of which, as has been well said, wore mitres.

Again, like Manning, he was in tune with the needs of the poor and was closer to the people than either Bourne or Vaughan had been, and he was praised for his human warmth, willingness to listen and less clericalist approach. It might be argued that his years in Africa had given him a more basic outlook and that he had a less triumphalist approach than most English Catholics, whose need to flaunt their self-proclaimed superiority is best seen in Archbishop Downey of Liverpool. At the time Downey was much more the image-maker of Catholicism in England than Hinsley, and he combined the battle for Catholic schools with plans to build the greatest (or at least the biggest) cathedral ever envisaged in the country.[19]

While Hinsley kept to his word about not allowing appeals for the decoration of the Cathedral, the work continued and had the Cardinal's full approval. What seems to have happened is that he found that there were large sums of money which had already been given for the work and which could not be used for anything else; in these circumstances there was no point in not continuing, whatever people might think about the 'luxury work'. The funds could be divided into two categories: monies left for specific projects, and monies left for the completion of the Cathedral in general. The former category contained the most – a total at the end of 1938 of nearly £19,000 in securities and £8,600 in the bank. The purposes for which the money had been bequeathed or given varied: to erect an outside altar (£25); an 'object in memory of Mgr Moyes' (£35); shrines to St Winifred (£50), St Anthony of Padua (£10), St Francis Xavier (£100) and St Cecilia (£100); a picture, statue or mosaic of St Pancras (£250); and, of course, for the major chapels – nearly £9,000 for the Blessed Sacrament chapel, £6,000 for St Paul's, £8,000 for St George's, £2,500 for the Lady Chapel, and so on. For the completion of the Cathedral and its general decoration there was over £7,000 in securities and £8,000 in the bank, with another £8,000 to come from a very recent bequest. The sums were large, but the cost of decorative work, especially if mosaics were to be used, was equally so; when Boris Anrep, a noted mosaicist, had been asked to prepare designs for St Patrick's chapel in 1937, his estimate had come to £10,400 – too much, it was decided, to spend on one chapel, even with the prospect of Irish and American contributions. While Hinsley agreed that the monies should be spent, he was still keen to keep a sense of proportion and to scotch the more outlandish schemes.

His advisory committee was very active. Their first task was to decide what should be done with Pownall's unfinished mosaic work in the apse. In the end it was agreed that it should be removed, except for the border; in his note approving this Hinsley asked that where possible the work should be given to any of the original workmen who were still unemployed. The committee also recommended that Bentley's great crucifix should be replaced to hang over the sanctuary, and this was eventually done. These matters were relatively straightforward; much more difficult were two issues of principle, and these occupied the committee for a long time without ever being fully resolved. The first was the question of how far the bare brick of the walls and piers in the nave should be covered with marble, as Bentley had planned; the second revolved around the type of mosaic work to be used – should it contain detailed designs and figures, or should it be as simple as possible, providing mainly a gold background?[20]

Some of the piers had already been covered in green marble, and some members of the committee suggested that this work should be completed; others preferred the effect of the bare brick and opposed adding any further marbling. Edward Hutton argued that such views reflected a complete ignorance of Byzantine architecture: both Santa Sophia in Constantinople and San Vitale in Ravenna – 'the two finest Byzantine buildings in the world' – were covered with the very same marble as had been used in the Cathedral. Bentley, he continued, had been 'absolutely right', and they could not go wrong in continuing what he had begun. During 1938 the committee asked Sir Giles Gilbert Scott for his opinion (he was also invited to become a member of the committee itself). His reply to the question whether he agreed with those members who thought that the bare brick was more pleasing was a little ambiguous. He said that they should aim at achieving in marble and mosaic 'that effect of sombre dignity and unity which had been obtained from the brick'. He believed that the 'sober, dignified atmosphere was gradually being destroyed and broken up', because the marbles were too sharply contrasted; some were too cold in colour and so strongly veined that they broke the simple lines of the piers. Any marbles used should not be highly polished, and, in particular, bright whites should be avoided. It reads as though he would have preferred the simplicity of the brickwork, but felt that as the marbling had been started it should be kept as simple and uniform as possible. The issue of how far Bentley's intentions should be the guiding principle for later generations would continue to vex advisory committees for years to come.

Scott also gave his opinion about the type of mosaics to be used. There should be no decided or bright colouring in them; indeed, the colours should be sufficiently sombre 'to give the effect of toned blacks, and used with black, brown, white and gold'. The lines of the arches, he went on, could be brought out by using ornament done in black or dark brown mixed with gold. This could hardly have been more different from Bentley's vision and from what had been realized in the Holy Souls chapel under his direction. It is interesting that Eric Gill also argued for simplicity to be the guiding criterion in the use of mosaic work when he was asked to propose a design for the apse over the choir, though his arguments were different from Scott's. It was because the art of mosaic working was neither native to England nor commonly practised there that he felt that it would be undesirable to use an elaborate pictorial manner. Moreover, while a great figure of Our Lord in glory flanked by the saints would be ideal in 'medieval Ravenna', such figures were no longer in keeping with the temper of the times. Therefore, he believed, the mosaic of the apse should be just a plain gold background, with a text in fine Roman letters, preferably in English, saying simply 'Praise be to God'; this would provide the best background to the hanging Crucifix, and the slight glint of light reflected from the tesserae would show up the contour of the half done. He went on to argue that if such a simple scheme were followed throughout the Cathedral, then its great beauty and dignity would be enhanced, whereas elaborate figures might damage its scale and proportions.

Gill changed his approach a little while later when he was asked to suggest a design for the tympanum over the high altar. He felt that an exception might be made here, and suggested a scene depicting the Palm Sunday procession on the left-hand side, the carrying of the cross on the right, and, in the centre, an angel holding a chalice from which the Precious Blood flowed (the Cathedral was dedicated to the Precious Blood). Even here, however, the scenes were not to be pictorial; the figures should be shown by means of a simple outline (in most cases black) on a gold background – the figures would thus be a 'kind of inscription'. He argued that the key message to be got across was one of poverty and humility, hence the concentration on Our Lord's suffering and humiliation. He ended with a plea: the Cathedral was a 'great big Church, in the midst of a great big Babylon. But it is not as a victor and as a swaggering Lord that we should appear. We must make an end of our complacence and give up bragging about our numbers and our world-wide influence.'[21] The advisory committee turned down this novel approach to mosaic work; Gill expressed his relief that he did not have to put his ideas into practice, and got on instead with the designing of an altarpiece for the chapel of St George and the English Martyrs for which he had been commissioned.

When he died in 1940 the work was unfinished. It was to depict Christ the

Priest on the Cross, flanked by the recently canonized Sts Thomas More and John Fisher. It was completed by Laurie Cribb, but was not installed until the war was over. When it was revealed to the public it caused controversy, not, as with the Stations, because of its style but because it had been altered. Gill had shown a pet monkey by the side of St Thomas More; this had apparently bothered the Cathedral authorities and so they had had the animal removed, leaving a slight imbalance in the finished work. Those who criticised the authorities' action made the obvious points: a work of art should not be tampered with after the artist's death (not even his widow had been told about the change), and animals were commonly shown in Christian art (for an obvious example, there were the ox and the ass in the crib). Others claimed that Gill had put in the monkey to show the inclusion of the whole of creation in Christ's redemptive work, and that in some way it was meant to be a protest at the lavish spending on 'meaningless and extravagant marbles' throughout the Cathedral. There were those, however, who supported the disappearance of the monkey: while animals might be acceptable in the crib, they would be out of place in a Crucifixion – especially a monkey, which usually raised a smile; others wondered whether the monkey had been in the original approved sketch. Perhaps the last word should be left with Gill. In another context he wrote that if a man bought one of his statues and did not like a part of it, then he would be free to remove that part or alter it 'or do anything he jolly well pleases'. He went on to decry as 'flat nonsense' talk of the 'sanctity of the work of artists', as though they were somehow inspired by the Holy Ghost. Gill the craftsman had a realistic appreciation of the position of the patron. He had already made it very clear that artistic work in the Cathedral (its 'furniture') must be subservient to the overall devotional purpose of the building; it would be deplorable, he felt, if it became the occasion for people to go sightseeing there as they did in Westminster Abbey.[22]

Early in 1939 Cardinal Hinsley asked that the work for which specific donations had been given should go ahead as soon as possible, and he gave permission for the release of the capital monies involved. The Committee drew up a list: St Joseph's chapel should be completed, likewise the floor in St Paul's chapel, and the north aisle should be lined with marble to match the south aisle; new designs for the choir apse and tympanum mosaics should be sought. The outbreak of war did not interrupt the work, and in April 1940, the committee announced detailed plans for the completion of the marbling in the north and south aisles; these included removing the green cipollino marble from six of the large piers in the nave and reusing it in the aisles – the nave piers would then show nothing but brick, and the committee attached great importance to this part of the plan, as it would do away with the 'patchwork' appearance of the nave and open the way for a free discussion of the right treatment of this part of the building. Hinsley agreed to the plans, but refused to allow what he referred to as 'demolition' work. By June, however, it was decided that the risk of war damage was too great to continue with any marbling, and steps were taken to protect the mosaic and marble floors of the chapels with wooden coverings. The contractors for the recent marble work, Messrs Fenning and Company, arranged to have a lorry and six men ready 'at any hour of the day or night' to salvage the mosaics, marbles, etc., in case of bomb damage to the Cathedral.[23] No such drastic action was needed, although the building was hit at various times by firebombs, and other bombs which exploded nearby caused considerable damage to windows, turrets, Clergy House and the administrative buildings. Hinsley died in March 1943. Despite his early reservations, he had taken a genuine interest in the Cathedral and its decoration and had insisted on being kept informed of every development. He laid no claim to artistic knowledge himself, and had relied entirely on the advisory committee of experts. Their discussions revealed at times all the differences of opinion originally feared by Bourne when he had refused to set up a similar committee; overall, however, their value had been proved.

After the war Cardinal Griffin re-established the committee of artistic experts, which had lapsed on Hinsley's death after an unfortunate episode had caused another outcry in the national press. The administrator, Mgr Collingwood, had had one of the main pillars from the north transept, near the Blessed Sacrament chapel, removed (he claimed that it got in the way of processions), and replaced with a steel girder. The marble for the pillar had been specially chosen by Bentley and came from the same quarry in Greece as that reputedly used in the building of Santa Sophia in Constantinople. There was also artistic dissatisfaction with some of the marbling which had been done in the sanctuary. The protest was again organized by Edward Hutton and signed by notables from the art world.[24]

The Cardinal appointed a new administrator, Gordon Wheeler, and this inaugurated a decade or so of very fruitful work on the decoration of the building which can be regarded as part of the heyday of the Cathedral in the 1950s and 1960s. Gordon Wheeler ranks as one of the outstanding administrators in the history of the Cathedral. He had great ability, ambitious ideas and a dedication to the Cathedral and all aspects of its work which was based on a deep belief in the Vaughan vision. With money from the previous donations and bequests and from the Cardinal's 'Million Crown Fund' appeal, he pushed forward the mosaic and marble decoration of the building. Two more chapels were completed, the marble revetment (or covering of the walls) was finished to a uniform height as well as the balustrades along the galleries. In all this Wheeler tried to keep to Bentley's designs and ideas as far as possible.

There was still considerable disquiet about the Pownall mosaics over the sanctuary. The committee urged that they should be replaced, and suggested the noted mosaicist, Boris Anrep, for the work. He had done his first work in the Cathedral as long ago as 1914, when he had designed the mosaics for the vault of the crypt; only a small part of this had been completed before the artist had gone off to the war, and it was not continued afterwards. In 1924 he had designed and executed the panel to St Oliver Plunkett which is in the south aisle between the chapels of St Gregory and St Patrick. When the Cardinal agreed to the removal of the Pownall mosaics one of the committee wrote to him to express his 'great joy' and to praise the Cardinal's courage in deciding to 'destroy what had been done with such good intentions'. Wheeler thought that the cost would be about £10,000, and that this could be met. When Anrep's estimate for his work alone (not including scaffolding and other essential costs) came to over £25,000, it was decided that the work could not be done and the scheme was dropped. It was pointed out to the committee that people would be very reluctant to give money to an appeal if it were to become known that it was to be spent on removing decoration already in place and paid for – and which, it might have been added, they did not share artistic scruples about.[25]

Attention turned to the task of completing the Blessed Sacrament chapel by adding mosaics. The commission was given to Anrep, largely at the instigation of Sir John Rothenstein, a member of the committee. The mosaics were to cover the whole of the chapel above its marble revetment and were designed to illustrate themes traditionally associated with the Trinity and the Eucharist. When the work was completed it was claimed that here was mosaic work close to 'the great tradition' of Ravenna and other ancient churches – unlike the work of Pownall in the Lady Chapel, for example, which was decorative and colourful but little more than illustration.[26]

It is worth describing here something of the processes involved in completing such a task – if nothing else it will help to explain the length of time and the high costs involved. After Anrep's initial sketches of the design had been accepted in 1956, he made full-sized colour cartoons and working drawings in his studio in Paris. These were used to put together the mosaic materials, which was done in Venice in the workshops of Angelo Orsoni who was also responsible for making the tesserae or small pieces of marble and other materials (for example, glass and mother of pearl) used. The final arrangement of the mosaic was, of course, done in the chapel itself as the pieces were being fixed – in this Anrep was helped by Justin Vulliamy, his artistic and technical assistant; the fixing was done by Peter Indri. The fixing was started in November 1960, and completed in December of the following year.[27]

And the cost? By February 1960, Anrep had already been paid £18,164 of the total of £39,500 due to him. This did not include the preparatory work which had to be done for the fixing, which came to about £4,000. Wheeler was concerned where the rest of the money (approximately £25,000 in all) was to come from, as the 'Million Crown Fund' was already overdrawn, and especially as Anrep was working more quickly than expected and so the final payments would have to be made earlier than planned for. So this one chapel (admittedly a very large one) needed about £45,000 to have its decoration completed – and that did not include the cost of the marble work which had already been done. At the same time, the marble revetment and the balustrading on the right-hand side of the nave was being worked on; this was costing over £8,000 for each of the half-bays of the transept, and over £6,000 for each of the other half-bays. It is understandable, then, that Cardinal Godfrey (who had succeeded Griffin in 1956) should have been even more than usually cautious when it was suggested that the work should be extended to complete the left-hand side as well.[28]

There was enough money from a former legacy, however, for the completion of another chapel, that dedicated to St Paul. The Advisory Art Committee rejected a scheme for this which had been drawn up by Aelred Bartlett, the brother of the future Administrator, whose help and advice had been very important in the marbling which had been completed. Instead they accepted a proposal by Boris Anrep according to which the mosaic decoration was designed and executed by Justin Vulliamy, with the advice and co-operation of Anrep himself who was responsible for the detailing of the principal figures. In the end, money was also found for the completion of the marble revetment on both sides of the nave and of the balustrade.[29]

All of this was not achieved without disagreement, of course. Some of this was due to inevitable differences of artistic judgement on particular issues, but there also emerged a basic difference of principle. This was the same question which had troubled Hinsley's committee: how far should Bentley's 'mind' continue to be the guiding criterion in deciding what should be done?

The issue surfaced again in 1955, just before an appeal for funds was to be launched: Wheeler believed that it was essential to be clear whether the money was being asked for in order to complete Bentley's designs or not. He and his sub-administrator Francis Bartlett were in favour of what may be called the Bentley approach, but others on the committee were not, most notably Sir John Rothenstein. He argued at a meeting in 1955 that since 'by Divine accident' Bentley's brickwork had 'emerged as so sublime a feature', the nave should be left as bare as possible and without any marble revetment. He lost that particular argument, and so did one of his supporters on the committee, Arthur Pollen, when in the following year he argued for the abandoning of Bentley's design for the marble balustrade. Rothenstein returned to the issue at a later meeting with the interesting argument that the 'austere bareness of the brickwork [was] so expressive of Northern Catholicism'; whether he was trying to say that Bentley, as a Yorkshireman, would have approved of its being left bare is not clear. He returned to the attack later by saying that Bentley, although a very great architect, was not always a great decorator; the present schemes (the marble revetment and the balustrade) would, he believed, impair rather than add to the beauty of the whole, and would also reduce the possibility of getting artists to 'execute really fine original works of art in the side chapels' – presumably because of the dominance of the colours of the marbles.[30]

The reference to 'fine original works of art' is interesting. At one stage, when the committee was discussing the decoration of the baptistery, Rothenstein suggested that the sculptor Henry Moore be approached to design mosaics. He argued that there was a 'magnificent austere dignity and exquisite colour' in Moore's drawings, and designs by him might make the baptistery a place of pilgrimage comparable to the Matisse chapel at Vence. Wheeler was immediately on his guard: the last thing that was wanted (he wrote to Francis Bartlett) was for the baptistery to become 'yet another piece of egoism instead of a part of a whole'. His reaction was in line with his rejection of concert performances in the Cathedral: it was essentially a house of prayer, and all its decoration and furnishings must help towards the realization of that function. He was not against using major artists and, indeed, always tried to get the best; perhaps he felt that Moore would have been just too individualistic. The sculptor was approached some years later when the question of completing the baptistery was again being discussed, but, after consideration, he decided that he was unable to submit designs for it.[31]

By the time Wheeler left Westminster in 1964 to become Coadjutor Bishop in Middlesbrough, the decoration of the Cathedral as it is today was essentially finished. Much of the credit for this achievement must go to Wheeler himself, for it is always the Administrator who sets the tone, as it were, for what is done in the Cathedral and it is abundantly clear that Wheeler had taken a close and knowledgeable interest in the various artistic projects during his term of office. He had negotiated both with the Cardinal of the day and with the Advisory Committee, sometimes initiating schemes, sometimes supporting those of others. He was later to insist that a greater debt was owed to Canon Francis Bartlett, his sub-Administrator. According to Wheeler it was the two brothers, Francis and Aelred Bartlett, who had worked out the best way of completing the marbling, and had travelled to Greece and elsewhere to choose the stone to be used. They had visited Santa Sophia in Constantinople, as well as Sicily and Ravenna to study the mosaics. He also claimed that it was they who had persuaded the Art Committee to have the balustrading done according to Bentley's original design. Some credence is given to this account of the Bartletts' influence by a reading of the correspondence surrounding the activity of the Advisory Art Committee, though not all its members welcomed the extent of that influence, particularly with Cardinal Godfrey, and there were tensions between the artistic experts and the amateurs.[32]

As well as the major work of the balustrading and the marble revetment, and the mosaics in the Blessed Sacrament and St Paul's chapels, it is worth noting two works of art which were erected in the Cathedral during Wheeler's period as Administrator – again, he gave much of the credit to Francis Bartlett. Giacomo Manzù, a controversial artist in his native Italy who had just completed a set of bronze doors for St Peter's in Rome, was commissioned to produce a relief of St Thérèse of Lisieux (to whom Cardinal Griffin had a special devotion). This interesting piece replaced an earlier unsatisfactory mosaic portrait of the saint. Then there is the beautiful fifteenth-century alabaster statue of Our Lady, known today as Our Lady of Westminster. The statue had been spotted at an antique dealers fair, and Cardinal Griffin was so keen to have it for the Cathedral that he gave Wheeler a cheque to buy it straight away. Wheeler found out, however, that the Dean of York Minster had already spoken for it and was starting a subscription list to buy it. The appeal fell flat and there was no public support for buying the statue for the Minster. Knowing of Wheeler's continued interest, the Dean wrote a few months later to say that he thought Westminster should be allowed to buy the statue. When it was installed in the Cathedral in a new shrine to Our Lady the Dean was represented at the ceremony – a nice ecumenical touch which owed much to Wheeler's good relations with other Christians.[33]

The cost of completing the mosaics for a single chapel was becoming prohibitive, and any thought of ever covering the vast domes as Bentley had intended had been out of the question almost from the beginning; as Wheeler wrote later, that particular problem, which exercised the minds of the Advisory Art Committee on a number of occasions, would only be solved by the invention of a successful mosaic spray! In the meantime, the committee turned its attention again to the baptistery. In 1966 the new Administrator, Mgr Tomlinson, had received designs for the mosaics from an Italian artist, Avenali, and for the marble revetment of the baptistery from Aelred Bartlett. Before the Advisory Committee made its decision about these, Tomlinson felt that its membership should be strengthened by the addition of Eustace Remnant, a retired architect who was an expert on the mosaics at Ravenna, and John Beckwith of the Victoria and Albert Museum, a noted Byzantinist. In writing to Cardinal Heenan to have these appointments approved he said that the committee for some time had not had enough specialized knowledge of Byzantine art and architecture: while he did not want the museum to become 'a kind of antique shop', it was important to maintain 'something of the Byzantine tradition' in its decoration. He had himself been to Ravenna to examine the mosaics and to talk to the artists working there. In the event, the Advisory Committee (including its new Byzantinists) were divided: some favoured the Avenali designs, others thought that it would be better to avoid anything pictorial and to cover the vault with plain mosaics and some simple floral decoration.[34]

The Italian designs were shown to Bentley's daughter and learned biographer, Winefride de l'Hopital. She wrote to the Cardinal that on seeing them she was full of hope that 'at last' the intentions of the architect, that the mosaics of the Cathedral should be in the 'vigorous Byzantine technique', were to be carried out. Those intentions could be seen realized in the Chapel of the Holy Souls where the mosaics had been designed 'under his close scrutiny'. She also felt that the sketches which she had been shown would be in harmony with the simple grandeur of Bentley's great baptismal font.[35] She was to be disappointed. It seems that Avenali lost interest because of the delays and withdrew. Five years later, in 1972, the Advisory Art Committee were still discussing the possibility of getting a mosaicist to take on the work; in the meantime the areas of the baptistery not covered in marble had been whitewashed. After that the finances of the Cathedral were in so precarious a state that finding money for further decorative work was out of the question, unless specific bequests or donations were received for the purpose, and even these became less likely as changes in liturgical thinking put the stress on simplicity of worship, and Christian concern for the disadvantaged came to the fore. Manning, not Vaughan and Wheeler, ruled, and aesthetic arguments and debates about how far Bentley's 'mind' should be followed gave way to financial considerations.

Much more could have been said in this chapter about the work of decorating the Cathedral. The marbles are magnificent, with about a hundred varieties from many countries – Ireland, Greece, Yugoslavia, Italy, France, Belgium, Algeria, Tunisia and Canada. They have been described as the ideal accompaniment to the architecture of the building in that they are smooth and do not introduce anything small or distracting, unlike some of the mosaic work; at the same time they are marvellous in their variety of shading and pattern, and add colour and warmth despite their natural coolness.[36] The metalwork is also of great interest, from the grilles of the various chapels to the screens and lighting pendants (called 'electroliers' when they were first installed), and there is also some fine woodwork and carving. The carved stone capitals of the columns show Bentley's attention to detail and his inventiveness as a craftsman at their best; the intricacies and lace-like lightness of some of this stonework is outstanding. Not all of this decoration was Byzantine, though we have seen that often there were genuine attempts to follow that rather elusive style which even the experts differed about. Nor, certainly, would Bentley have accepted or admired everything that was to done to his building. Yet the Cathedral is something more than the sum of its parts, and if there are details which appear to modern taste to be unfortunate they do not detract from the experience of the whole; and who knows what will be acceptable to those who visit it or pray in it a generation or so from now?

To finish with, something must be said about the outside of the building. With the exception of the tympanum over the main west door (completed in 1916) the external decoration of the Cathedral was more or less complete by the time of Bentley's death in 1902. The most important change to affect the outside of the building since then was undoubtedly the opening up of sufficient space in front of the building to provide a full view of the façade. Westminster City Council and the Church Commissioners (who owned the land and were willing to lease it to the Council at a nominal rent) approved a scheme for a large piazza in front of the Cathedral, suitably paved to match Bentley's general colour scheme for the outside of the building. It was officially opened in December 1975. It is interesting that had such a space existed originally then the front elevation of the building would have looked quite different, for the surrounding houses were so close that Bentley had run into problems over their rights 'to light and air' at the planning stage. After taking legal advice he had to make considerable alterations which affected the façade and the position of the campanile. The west front was 'stepped', so that the tall western end of the first of the great nave bays was set forty feet further back than the main entrance, and the campanile was similarly realigned. The existence of the piazza, and the cleaning of the external fabric, have allowed the Cathedral to become closer to being the striking spiritual symbol in the heart of the capital which Vaughan had in mind.[37]

Before ending this chapter on the decoration of the Cathedral something should be said about the recent cleaning of the interior, especially of the mosaics. This has been carried out with the help of funds from English Heritage and the effect is remarkable. One has only to look at the very recently cleaned chapel of the Holy Souls (finished in November 1993) to be struck by the beauty of the colours, especially of the silver in the vault, and to realize, again, the genius of Bentley's vision. Present-day religious sensitivities do not respond to the symbolism in these mosaics as readily as in Bentley's time, but there is a lasting quality which calls the Christian viewer to serious thought. Bentley may have spoken of the mosaics and the marbles as a veneer on the main structure of his building, but neither are superficial to its main purpose of being a house of prayer. And what has been left undone in the domes has, perhaps, to the modern eye a sense of mystery which complements the beauty and atmosphere of the rest.

NOTES

1   J. G. Snead-Cox, *The Life of Cardinal Vaughan* (1912), II, pp. 345–6.
2   E. Oldmeadow, *Francis Cardinal Bourne* (1940, 1944), I, p. 259.
3   See G. Bovini, *Ravenna Mosaics* (1957), pp. 44–5.
4   A. Derrick, 'Westminster Cathedral', *The Tablet* (2 May 1982), pp. 449–50; W. de l'Hopital, *Westminster Cathedral and Its Architect* (1919), I, pp. 198ff, 246ff.
5   D. l'Hopital, I, pp. 152–62. There's a story in Maisie Ward's *Insurrection Versus Resurrection*, vol. 2 (1938), pp. 149–50, about Bourne sending his architect Marshall to study the mosaics in Italy for four months; it was at a heated dinner discussion, when the Archbishop was subjected to ill-concealed scorn by some of the art experts of the day. It was Bourne, not Marshall, who went.
6   De l'Hopital, I, pp. 173–4 (Lady Chapel), 256–8 (tympanum).
7   De l'Hopital, I, pp. 163–7; G. Stamp, *Robert Weir Schultz, Architect, and His Work for the Marquess of Bute* (Mount Stewart, 1981), pp. 60ff.

8   W. R. Lethaby (ed.), *Ernest Gimson, His Life and Work* (London/Stratford/Oxford, 1924). Mgr Francis Bartlett, who was extremely knowledgeable about the Cathedral decorations and furnishings, supported the bog oak tradition: see S. and E. Usherwood, *Friends Newsletter* (Spring 1991) and letter to the author (October 1993); N. Pevsner, *The Buildings of England: London*, 1: *The Cities of London and Westminster* (3rd edn, 1973), p. 483.

9   E. Gill, *Autobiography* (1940), pp. 200–1; AAW, Bo 1/24c; the issue was very controversial.

10   M. Yorke, *Eric Gill, Man of Flesh and Spirit* (1981), pp. 202–4.

11   For opposition, see AAW, 'Cathedral Files II', folder on St Andrew's chapel. On Gill's figures, see McGreevy, quoted in Yorke, pp. 206–7.

12   *Westminster Cathedral Chronicle* (1918), pp. 50–3, where Gill writes under the name of E. Rowton (his second name).

13   Pevsner, p. 482; D. Peace, *Friends Newsletter* (Autumn 1985 and Spring 1986).

14   *Cathedral Chronicle* (1934), pp. 1ff., for Bourne's article.

15   *The Daily Telegraph*, letters from Hutton (7 December 1933 and 6 August 1934).

16   *Cathedral Chronicle* (January 1934), p. 4, for attack on Hutton; papers and letters in AAW, Bo 1/24c, and 'Cathedral Files II'; articles in *The Evening Standard* and *The Manchester Guardian* (3 December 1935).

17   AAW, 'Cathedral Files II'. F. Bartlett's unpublished paper on 'The Cathedral marbles' is useful; I am grateful to Miss E. Brown for kindly giving me a copy.

18   AAW, 'Cathedral Files II', Hinsley to Myers (December 1935); Hi 3, 'Cathedral 1935–41', Hinsley to Hirst (9 October 1935).

19   T. Moloney, *Westminster, Whitehall and the Vatican: The Role of Cardinal Hinsley 1935–1943* (1985), pp. 154, 156; G.A. Beck (ed.), *The English Catholics 1850–1950* (1950), pp. 173–4, on Cardinal Bourne; A. Hastings, *A History of English Christianity 1920–1985* (1987), p. 275.

20   AAW, Hi 3, 'Cathedral 1935–41'.

21   Ibid., Paper, 'Sir Giles G. Scott's opinion'. Eric Gill submitted a number of proposals in October and November 1938.

22   AAW, box file 'Westminster Cathedral', has a full summary of the controversy as it appeared in the *Catholic Herald*, by Miss E. Poyser, former archivist. See also M. Yorke, p. 210, and D. Peace, *Friends Newsletter* (Spring 1988).

23   AAW, box file, 'Westminster Cathedral', folder 'Various Chapels 1935–41'.

24   The best source for these years is the Goodhart-Rendell papers in the British Architectural Library (RIBA), file 'Catholic Art Committee'; I am grateful to Peter Howell for this information. H. S. Goodhart-Rendell became a Catholic in 1924, was Slade Professor of Fine Art at Oxford and Vice-Chairman of the RIBA; he was a member of Hinsley's Advisory Art Committee. There are two folders, G-ReH/12/1/1 (September 1953–December 1955), and G-ReH/12/2/1 (January 1956–April 1959).

25   RIBA, G-ReH/12/1: Goodhart-Rendell to Cardinal (4 November, 5 November 1954), for Wheeler on Anrep's costs.

26   F. Bartlett in *Chronicle* (July 1969).

27   G. Wheeler's booklet, *Westminster Cathedral, The Blessed Sacrament Chapel Mosaics* (1962); and article by J. Vulliamy, 'Some reflections on mosaic decoration', *Friends Newsletter* (Autumn 1987).

28   AAW, Go 2/22 (1960–61), Wheeler to Canon Rivers (22 February 1960), and to Godfrey (14 June 1960), Godfrey to Wheeler (11 July 1960).

29   Booklet (by Wheeler?), *Westminster Cathedral – The St Paul's Chapel Mosaics* (n.d.).

30   RIBA, G-ReH/12/1 (18 May and 10 June 1955) and 12/2 (25 April 1956).

31 RIBA, G-ReH/12/1: discussions of September 1955. For the baptistery, AAW, Tomlinson to Heenan (12 September 1966 and 19 April 1967).

32 See Wheeler's panegyric of Mgr Bartlett, *Friends Newsletter* (Autumn 1992).

33 Author's interview with Bishop Wheeler (September 1992) and the Bishop's *In Truth and Love* (Leeds, 1990), pp. 68–9.

34 Tomlinson letters as in note 31 above.

35 AAW, W. de l'Hopital to Cardinal Heenan (16 April 1967).

36 Pevsner, pp. 481–2; Bartlett, *Friends Newsletter* (Spring 1989).

37 Howell, *Architectural History* (1982), pp. 81–2; de l'Hopital, I, pp. 56–7, 100; *The Tablet* (13 December 1975), p. 1224.

Chapter 6

Close to the ideal:
1945 to 1965

To PICK OUT A CERTAIN PERIOD as a golden age can often be tempting but is usually mistaken, for it involves a judgement on the past from the standpoint of a less enjoyable or successful present, when the criterion for the judgement is what is happening now rather than what was happening at the time in question. If such a judgement is made about the Cathedral in the twenty years or so after the Second World War, then there is a major risk that those making the judgement are doing so because they dislike the changes that followed a period of apparent calm and security. Yet, as has been seen already, these were years which witnessed genuine achievements: the success of the music under George Malcolm, for example, and the work done to carry forward the decoration of the building. It was also a time when the pastoral mission of the Cathedral was developed further than ever before, and a range of liturgical changes implemented and absorbed successfully. Before we go on to look at some of these things in detail, something will be said about the general position of English Catholicism at the time.

A recent historian has claimed that the Catholic Church was unique in England in the years after 1920 in that it continued to consolidate and even expand its position at a time when all the other major churches were declining. By 1950 it had developed a sizeable middle-class constituency, had no longer to fight for recognition of its educational claims and was spreading outside its traditional centres in the industrial north and midlands to give it a more even geographical representation. New churches were being built, vocations to the priesthood were high and overall about 10 per cent of the population could be classed as practising Catholics.[1] The diocese of Westminster was sharing in this growth. Its estimated Catholic population of 300,000 in 1940 had risen to 470,000 in 1960; churches and chapels open to the public had increased from 196 to 212, and while the number of secular clergy had risen only very slighly, the number of regulars had jumped from 270 to 390. Marriages in Catholic churches had numbered just under 4,500 in 1938; in 1958 they numbered over 7,500. Conversions to Catholicism rose in the same period from 1,400 to 1,900 per year.[2]

Was there a change in attitudes to accompany this increase in numbers and an easier acceptance by English society as a whole? The answer is, probably not. The old fortress mentality may have been slowly fading away as Catholics became more secure, but acceptance did not mean integration with the rest of society; nor was this the aim. Mixed marriages were still severely frowned on, there was no relaxing of the prohibition on Catholic parents' sending their children to non-Catholic schools, the seminaries were still as isolated as ever from the mainstream of higher education and the tender shoots of ecumenism which had begun to appear under Cardinal Hinsley had not been encouraged by his successors Griffin and Godfrey. Indeed, the feeling of security was based not so much on any acceptance by the larger community around them as on the certainty of their own beliefs and practice. There were, of course, some changes beginning to take place: one example was a small new journal called simply *Scripture*: this was trying to move English Catholic biblical scholarship into new ways of thinking more in line with recent papal pronouncements and Continental scholarship. It was edited from the seminary at Upholland, where Fr Alec Jones was also starting work on the massive translation of the scholarly Jerusalem Bible. But the fruits of these and other worthwhile initiatives were not to be gathered until several years later. In the 1950s English Catholics may 'never have had it so good', as Hastings claims, but they were enjoying their good fortune quietly – and even a little smugly.

This, then, was the background to what was happening at the Cathedral – the musical revival under Malcolm, the efforts to ensure the proper performance of the unchanging daily liturgy of the Church in all its traditional richness and to finish as much of the decoration of the building as possible. But Vaughan and those who followed him and shared his vision had not wanted a Cathedral set in aspic, no matter how perfect it might be. As pointed out already, there had from the start been a tension between the Cathedral's liturgical demands and the traditional pastoral outlook of the majority of the priests who served it; the tension could sometimes be inhibiting, but at other times it ensured that as far as possible the Cathedral got the best of both approaches – whatever the strains on individual priests which this may have imposed. Gordon Wheeler was no cloistered Dean; he understood the demands of the Cathedral's pastoral mission not just to its own parishioners but also to the many hundreds of people who used it regularly as their place of worship, and to the large numbers who 'dropped in' from time to time for Mass, the sacraments, the music or just for anonymous advice or comfort. The differing needs of such a congregation called for an imaginative and varied response on the part of the Cathedral authorities.

Something should be said here about the Cathedral parish. The northern part of it consists of a number of parks and open spaces – St James's Park, Green Park and Buckingham Palace Gardens. Boundaries run along Pall Mall, Whitehall, the river Thames between Westminster and Vauxhall Bridges, Vauxhall Bridge Road, around Victoria Station and then up Grosvenor Place to Hyde Park Corner. It is, socially, a very mixed area with extremes of wealth and poverty; it has a large percentage of semi-permanent residents and a high proportion of bed-sit and multi-occupation accommodation. In 1901 the area had 39,517 resident inhabitants; this had dropped to 16,383 by 1971. Despite the decrease, the area still had one of the highest population densities in the country, at 180 people to the acre. It is difficult to get accurate estimates of the number of Catholics living within the parish boundaries (as opposed to those attending Mass at the Cathedral) over the years; a survey in 1978 gave a figure of 1,700.[3] From 1910 the parish had been divided into a number of districts (five to begin with, later increased to thirteen) and the choir Chaplains were given the responsibility for their pastoral care.

It was a large parish in area, and for some years before the 1950s there had been a feeling that parts of it were too distant for the people to be able to get to the Cathedral easily or for them to build up that almost proprietorial relationship with it that characterized so many urban Catholic parishes – perhaps the nature and size of the building itself also militated against this. There were two areas in particular where the people seemed to feel cut off – Pimlico and the Horseferry Road area. Chapels of ease had been established in both, and when a new church was built in Pimlico in 1957 the obvious step was to establish it as a separate parish. One of the arguments which Wheeler used in support of this was that the increase of pastoral activity at the Cathedral had made regular visiting of the Catholics in Pimlico even more difficult for the Chaplains to carry out; the people would respond much more readily to priests who were actually in their midst. The other part of the Cathedral parish which he thought should have its own church and be made into a separate parish was the Horseferry Road area, otherwise known as the Millbank Estate. There had been a parish there in the nineteenth century, with its own church, St Mary's. Cardinal Vaughan, apparently afraid that the Cathedral might not be used enough, closed St Mary's and ordered that it be replaced as parish church by the Cathedral. It seems that the local people failed to adopt it as their church, and so various attempts had been made over the years to open a permanent church in the area, usually connected with a convent of nuns, but none had been successful. Wheeler wrote to the Cardinal in 1957 that he was always on the look-out for a suitable site, but the area was so built up and 'tightly planned by the London County Council' that he could do nothing. In 1962 a new church was built for the Sisters in the Corpus Domini Convent, and this, in effect, became the parish church for the area, served by a Marist priest although technically still a chapel of ease of the Cathedral.[4]

One of the pastoral activities which Wheeler had referred to as increasing was that of the confessional. When he had been a Chaplain there he had seen that there were great possibilities to develop this side of the Cathedral's work, and when he became Administrator he set about organizing matters so that there was always at least one priest either in a confessional or easily on call. As he admitted, this could not have been achieved without a strong commitment on the part of the Chaplains. He claimed that it brought new life to the building because there were always queues of people waiting for confession. So heavy was the demand, indeed, that Wheeler wrote to the Cardinal to ask if some of the regular clergy who worked in the diocese might not help out, to avoid one priest's being 'in the box' from 2 p.m. to 6 p.m.; the Jesuits might take one day, the Redemptorists another, the Passionists another, and so on. The superiors of the religious orders were in favour, but Godfrey was not: in such important and regular work, he wrote, he did not want to be dependent on the help of the religious orders.[5]

It is clear from the testimony of the Cathedral Chaplains themselves that they regarded this confessional work as most important, and at least for some of them it served as a welcome break from the singing of the Office. Fr Michael Hollings, for example, was one of those appointed without any regard to the fact that he could not sing and the ceremonies of the official liturgy had little appeal for him. He was instrumental in developing the unofficial pastoral side of the Cathedral's mission, partly through the confessional but also in just being available at the back of the Cathedral to meet and talk to people and so to break down the inevitable barrier which a highly formalized liturgy created between the congregation and the clergy. In this way he made contact with those needing help and developed a ministry which was of great value to Catholics and non-Catholics alike. There were still tensions between the two roles of choral Chaplain and district visitor; the priests worked a system of having alternate weeks doing each job and it was not easy to be dealing with, say, a delicate pastoral problem in one's district and not to be readily available to the parishioner concerned while one went off to sing the Office in the Cathedral.[6] No doubt this 'unofficial' pastoral work had been done before; what seems to have happened while Wheeler was in charge was that it became more regular and accepted as part of the Cathedral's mission. Perhaps what was important here was not the individual activities but the general tone set by the Administrator. One change may be referred to here by way of illustration. There had formerly been an arrangement whereby anyone wanting to go to confession could ring a bell and a priest would come through into the Cathedral; Wheeler was convinced that for every person who rang the bell there were probably two or three others who would hesitate to do so, and to meet their needs it was better to have a priest sitting waiting in a confessional – and so the hours of attendance of a priest in a confessional were extended to cover the time when the Cathedral was open. This part of the pastoral ministry continues today, with the Cathedral providing 60 hours of confessions each week, including nine hours on a Sunday. And what other church anywhere, I wonder, provides four hours of confessions on Christmas morning?

While these changes, minor in themselves, were taking place at the Cathedral in the 1950s, there were others being introduced throughout the Church as a whole which marked the beginning of a liturgical revolution. The initial impetus for these had come from Pius XII's encyclical on the liturgy, *Mediator Dei*, which had been published in 1947. This had been the result of a movement for liturgical change which had been growing during the century. In the encyclical the Pope stressed the need to accept change as a sign of life within the Church. In particular, the role of the laity in the liturgy needed to be reinterpreted in the light of fresh thinking about the priesthood of all believers. The idea of congregational participation in the liturgy was not, of course, new – as we have seen, both Vaughan and Bentley had had it in mind when deciding on the style of building for the Cathedral. Now, however, it was to be far more radical because the idea for it had grown out of a theological reappraisal. The encyclical gave the liturgy its own theology to guide its development; change would not be for change's sake, as was often to be claimed by opponents of the reforms in the difficult years to come, but the result of a genuinely theological renewal.

When the revisions in the liturgy began to be implemented in the 1950s the changes that appeared most striking were the reduction in the fasting regulations before Holy Communion, and the introduction of the vernacular into the Church's official liturgy. The former meant that the need to fast from midnight was done away with; at first it was replaced by a period of fasting of three hours and later (in 1964) by one of only one hour. This led to the introduction of Masses in the evening and a major change in the traditional pattern of Sunday devotional practice. The Dialogue Mass in Latin was introduced to help congregational participation, and commentaries at Mass were encouraged as a way of instructing the people. In addition, and much more radically, the whole of the great Holy Week liturgy was revised: the vernacular was introduced for the first time, the involvement of the people was built in as an integral part of the new ceremonies and the rites themselves were fundamentally different.

Gordon Wheeler and the authorities at the Cathedral adopted a positive attitude to the changes, seeing in them a way of extending its pastoral mission without interfering with its liturgical one. Changes were introduced gradually. A Sunday evening Mass was started in January 1956, and permission for daily evening Mass was granted by the Cardinal in December 1957. As evening Masses are now so accepted a part of every parish's liturgical life, it is interesting to note the arguments which Wheeler had used to convince the Cardinal that the Cathedral should have one. He understood, he wrote, that in most of the capital cities of Europe there was at least one place where evening Mass was permitted, and he had learned that Venice and the Duomo at Florence had one, while Rome had at least two. He felt that it would be fully justified to have one in London, and that the Cathedral was the obvious place for it, since it was so central and used by so many people who worked nearby. He had no doubt that it would enable greater numbers of people to become daily communicants.

By March of the following year Wheeler was asking for and obtaining permission for a second evening Mass on holy days because so many were attending the one at 6 p.m. Dialogue Masses had been introduced some time earlier, but in a limited way; in 1959 Wheeler asked for these to be increased in number, and argued at the same time that the Cathedral should be giving a lead to other churches in the diocese about how best to implement the liturgical changes, just as it continued to give a lead in its performance of the more solemn Divine Office. Again the Cardinal granted permission, with the interesting comment that he hoped that the Dialogue Masses would not prove to be a distraction to priests who were saying their private Masses at the side altars. One of the problems about Dialogue Masses, according to Wheeler, lay in getting the celebrants to speak sufficiently clearly and slowly and in finding enough other priests willing to lead the people in their responses; would it be possible, he asked the Cardinal, to train a few lay people to do this? The Cardinal, however, was not keen, and stipulated that if it had to be done then the lay people should not be allowed to lead from the sanctuary.[7] There was in all this both Cardinal Godfrey's typical caution and Gordon Wheeler's concern to ensure that everything possible should be done to enable the Cathedral to serve the pastoral needs of its very mixed congregations.

One of the changes introduced as part of the liturgical reform was an insistence that every public Mass should include some form of catechetical instruction for the people. This created a minor problem at the Cathedral where there were a number of short, early Sunday morning Masses at half-hourly intervals starting at 6 a.m. This did not allow enough time for an instruction to be given, and so the Masses were rescheduled so that each could last 45 minutes. This meant cutting out the Mass at 6.30, and Wheeler was concerned that this might cause problems for the large number of nurses from the Westminster Hospital who had attended it. To make sure that they were still provided for he sought and obtained permission to have a Mass said at the hospital itself on Sundays and holy days; this would have the added advantage of being available for some of the patients and other staff as well as the nurses.[8] It was also, of course, another task for the Cathedral clergy who provided chaplains for the four hospitals within the parish boundaries; in addition to the Westminster, there were the Gordon Hospital, the Grosvenor Hospital for Women and the Westminster Children's Hospital.

On the whole these early reforms and changes did not affect the official liturgy of the Cathedral, which continued to centre on the daily singing of the Divine Office and the sung capitular Mass. There does not seem to have been any feeling that the gap between this liturgy and that provided for the people was bound to get wider the more changes were introduced into one and not the other. I say, 'on the whole', for there was one area in which the official liturgy was affected fundamentally by the new approach, and that was in the observance of Holy Week. The decree of November 1955 completely revised the rites in an attempt to restore a liturgical celebration which would allow the people to take a full part in the various services, instead of having to make do with the various extra-liturgical devotions which had grown up over the years as the official celebration had become increasingly the preserve of the clergy. The response of the Cathedral was, again, positive, and in an article in the *Cathedral Chronicle* for March 1956, George Malcolm explained the reasons for the reforms. The Church's aim, he wrote, was to give Holy Week back to the faithful as something vital and significant, so that it would become a truly corporate re-enactment of the events of Our Lord's last hours, and would 'evoke a readier response, a fuller participation'. What he called 'a great deal of dead wood' was cut away by the reforms, so that attention could be focused on the essentials. He was honest enough to admit that 'many cords of sentiment and tradition' were broken in the process, and that it might well take some time for the new Maundy Thursday to 'command our affections as it commands our obedience'. In particular, as Master of Music, he regretted the virtually total loss of *Tenebrae* as the occasion for so much fine music; but at the same time, he admired the firm decision of the new decree not to allow anything to deflect attention from the great liturgical actions of the Last Supper and the Crucifixion. Time alone would show, he concluded, whether the changes would rekindle people's zeal and promote fuller participation; in the meantime, the ideal demanded enthusiastic co-operation. In some ways Malcolm's sentiments may be taken as representative of those whose duty it was to implement the various changes. On the whole they probably preferred the tried and traditional, but their pastoral sense made them bring in the new, and this was done enthusiastically and not just dutifully.

Further changes in the Divine Office were introduced in 1961 which made minor differences to the demands on the Chaplains. The morning office of Matins and Lauds was no longer anticipated on the previous evening but recited at 8.30 a.m., with the other Hours and High Mass at 10.00 a.m. In the early evening there was sung Vespers at 5.00 p.m., followed by recited Compline and simple Benediction. Overall, the chaplains were left freer in the afternoon and evening than before – probably more useful times for their parochial duties.[9] A detailed breakdown of their various obligations about this time says that each Chaplain spent at least three hours one day a week in the confessional; in addition, the celebrant of each morning Mass was expected to hear confessions before or after his Mass. On Saturdays each had at least one and a half hours in the confessional, while on Sundays five priests had about forty minutes each, with another five sharing the duty for the rest of the day. Then there was 'door duty': for this the day was divided into two periods, from 9 a.m. to 4 p.m., and from 4 p.m. to 11 p.m. (with variations on Saturdays and Sundays); each priest did three to four periods on duty each month.[10] While one can understand the complaints of those Chaplains who were not 'liturgically minded' that their choral duties interfered with their pastoral work, the time taken up by them every other week does not seem too heavy.

No attempt to give a picture of the life of the Cathedral in these years could be successful unless it covered the multiplicity of societies and religious sodalities which were an integral part of every large and active Catholic parish in the post-war years. Liturgical reformers might argue that the existence of these bodies, which met an undoubted need in many Catholics, showed that the formal liturgy of the Church was failing to provide the full spiritual nourishment necessary to a healthy religious life. Certainly, most of this side of parish life has disappeared in the years since the major liturgical and other reforms of the Second Vatican Council, in some cases so completely that it is difficult to think oneself back into the English Catholic mentality of the earlier period. A look at a typical week's evening programme in the Cathedral will illustrate this. On Monday the Guild of Our Lady of Walsingham met and a sermon was preached followed by Benediction; the Guild's main purpose was to pray for the conversion of England to Catholicism. On Tuesday, the Confraternity of the Blessed Sacrament met, again with sermon and Benediction. On Wednesday there was a talk or instruction on the Catholic faith, followed by Benediction. On Thursday it was the turn of the Confraternity of the Apostleship of Prayer, with sermon and Benediction; the Confraternity existed to foster devotion to the Sacred Heart of Jesus. On Friday, the Confraternity of the Precious Blood had its devotions, followed by a sermon and Benediction, and, finally, on Saturday the Confraternity of the Holy Rosary met; again there was Benediction. From January 1952, the Monday slot was taken over by the Perpetual Novena in honour of Our Lady of the Miraculous Medal. The Children of Mary also met every week for devotions, while the Third Order of St Francis met on the first Sunday of each month for prayers, sermon and Benediction. There was also, of course, the ongoing devotion to the Sacred Heart expressed through the practice of receiving Holy Communion on nine successive first Fridays.

In addition to these devotional and prayer groups there were others which made up a more practical apostolate. The Legion of Mary was a popular form of Catholic Action and social service, and its members were active in visiting prisons and hospitals, following up lapsed Catholics, meeting Catholic immigrants at the main railway stations, organizing the distribution of Catholic literature, working with young people and, in general, being of assistance to the parish clergy. And then there was the St Vincent de Paul Society, or SVP, the main agent of charitable relief in any parish. Its work was built essentially on regular home visiting of the sick and the poor. It has to be remembered that the parish attached to the Cathedral was made up of a number of areas of contrasting wealth and poverty, from Belgravia at one end to Peabody estates at the other. Both these Catholic Action groups and those mentioned in the previous paragraph made demands on the clergy at the Cathedral: each had its chaplain who was expected to attend its weekly meetings and give sermons and Benediction as required. In addition, a number of the priests were responsible for visiting the local schools and taking religious instruction classes.

There was nothing unusual in all this – the same range of activities and pastoral concerns would have been found in any large, urban parish up or down the country. They are mentioned here because they help to complete the picture of Cathedral life, a picture which can easily be distorted if one concentrates on the more obvious features of its public image and official worship. Clearly, the authorities needed to strike a balance between the demands of the Cathedral's different roles, and the Administrator, in particular, had to be part diplomat, part parish priest and part managing director if he was to look after all these interests properly and ensure that each got its proper share of attention and resources.

There were, of course, the great occasions, such as the celebrations in 1950 to mark the centenary of the Restoration of the Hierarchy, and the solemn reception of Cardinal Godfrey in 1958. There were visits by VIPs and foreign heads of state, especially in the years after decolonization when some of the new states wished to celebrate their independence with a Mass in the Cathedral. In June 1961, President and Mrs Kennedy visited the Cathedral for the christening of their niece Anna Christina Radziwill, whose godfather was the President. It was a private occasion but involved a massive security operation; in addition, the Administrator had been involved in negotiations with the Princess Radziwill, the President's sister-in-law, who had wanted the ceremony to take place in her house on the analogy of royal christenings' being held at Buckingham Palace – neither Wheeler nor the Cardinal could see any reason for their not using the Cathedral in the normal way. There were also lesser 'state occasions': an annual 'Red Mass' for Catholic members of the legal profession, an academic Mass to mark the opening of each new university year, a Police Guild annual Requiem, and so on. The Cathedral was fulfilling its varied roles – as a centre for English Catholicism, a house of daily official and private prayer, and a local parish church.[11]

One other initiative introduced while Wheeler was Administrator should be mentioned here. In January 1955, the Church Unity Octave was observed for the first time in the Cathedral. The week was marked by special evening services and sermons by noted preachers; it ended with a Pontifical High Mass. It was a peculiarly Catholic affair: not only were all the preachers Catholic, but the title given to the week was the Chair of Unity Octave. Wheeler explained in an article in the *Cathedral Chronicle* that the purpose was 'to enquire into the relations between the Church and other Christian and non-Christian bodies, and to draw people to love the Chair of Unity which Our Lord had established'. Unity, to most Catholics in the 1950s, meant that other people would give up their errors and become Catholics. Attendances at the services were reported to be good. The week was observed again in the following year, this time with a slight change in its title to the Chair of Union Octave; the sermon on the final evening was 'The Chair of Union and the missionary conquest of the world for Christ'. In the initial notices about the octave people were urged to support 'this important octave so highly commended by the Pope'. It appears that attendances did not stay at the initial satisfactory levels. Perhaps the novelty was wearing off, for Wheeler had to admit in 1957 that the octave was 'dutifully rather than enthusiastically' attended. He felt that the authorities had not yet got the approach right to the people – perhaps it was the fault of the language used. 'The Chair of Union' was, he thought, a perplexing title to the uninitiated, and even 'octave' had an esoteric flavour. The one word which was clear and to which the people responded was 'mission' – would it be better to refer to the Unity Octave as the 'Epiphany Mission', with 'Chair of Union' as its sub-title and theme? He admitted that it was not just the language that was wrong: the talks had tended to become 'overlong disquisitions instead of assaults on our complacency'. The best talk, and the one best attended, in 1956 was, he reported, on the evening devoted to lapsed Catholics. It would be sad, he concluded, if English Catholics were to lag behind those in other countries, 'to say nothing of our separated brethren, in our desire . . . *ut sint unum*'. Elsewhere it was noted that attendance at the services in 1956 had been 'reasonably good', especially on those occasions when there was evening Mass.[12]

All this was a very long way from the heady spirit of ecumenism in the

1960s after the Second Vatican Council, and the great occasion in 1968 when Cardinal Heenan welcomed the Archbishop of Canterbury to the Cathedral to preach during the Unity Octave. Uncertainties about what to call the week of prayer, references to sessions devoted to lapsed Catholics and suggestions that it would be better to think of it as a 'mission', all tell their own tale. The week continued to be observed as the 'Chair of Union Octave', but little attention was given to it in the *Chronicle*, for example – indeed, in some years it did not even merit a mention in the list of Cathedral services. The people could hardly be expected to respond enthusiastically when the official policy was to discourage religious contacts between Catholics and other Christians and even to forbid them to say the 'Our Father' in common or to join in non-Catholic weddings and funerals; nor, indeed, would most of them respond enthusiastically to the major change in policy when it came in the 1960s, so thorough had been their previous grounding in the exclusivist party line. It should, perhaps be noted as a postscript here that the official visit of Archbishop Ramsey in 1968 was not his first visit to the Cathedral. While Wheeler was Administrator Ramsey had asked if he might make a private visit, and this was done after dark one evening when the Cathedral was closed, so that news of it would not get out. It was, apparently, a moving and emotional occasion, with the Archbishop and the Administrator praying side by side in the Blessed Sacrament chapel.[13]

The Second Vatican Council (1962–65) brought in further liturgical changes. But the background now was quite different, for the Council also examined all the other key aspects of the Church's life and mission, and so what was happening in the liturgy was only one part of a general revolution. The sources of authority in the Church, collegiality, the role of the priestly and religious life, relations with other churches, the role of the people of God, everything seemed to be open to question as the Council tried to 'read the signs of the times' and to accept complete renewal. Moreover, the change was not limited to the official documents issued by the Council: a new spirit of enquiry was released by the Council and remained long after its closure. There was, inevitably, confusion as both clergy and laity experimented; there were, also inevitably, those who opposed the changes and preferred the traditional securities. Many of the changes were implemented without enough being done to explain the reasons for them and to instruct people in the new theological insights which had led the Council to its conclusions. Talking of the liturgical changes, Adrian Hastings has written: 'all in all this was an immense revolution, carried through rapidly, smoothly, with typical Catholic discipline, but awfully little explanation or enthusiasm'. There was, perhaps, more enthusiasm among ordinary Catholics than he allows for, but they had certainly not been well prepared for it all.[14]

The main liturgical changes as they affected England are easily summarized. English was first introduced into the Mass in 1964, with a fully vernacular Mass following in 1967. Changes began to be made to the position of high altars, and concelebration came in. The most important change, however, was the introduction of the new *Missa Normativa* in 1970: most important because it changed the form of the Mass, allowing a variety of prayers of consecration and omitting altogether some of the traditional elements. These changes raised some fundamental issues in relation to the Cathedral and its role.

In the first place, much of the new liturgical thinking revolved around the idea of community: the liturgy should be a community's joint act of worship, both arising from and helping to form community. What was the Cathedral's community? For years the lack of a natural community and the ephemeral nature of most of its congregations had been accepted – and, indeed, given as a reason for lack of participation in the services. There was also the size of the building, which militated against a community feeling, and its design, which necessarily kept the people at a distance from the priest.

Then there was the question of the future of the daily capitular Mass and the singing of the Divine Office. The latter had not been left untouched by the changes and, as well as having been simplified, could now be said in the vernacular. How would this affect its performance in the Cathedral? It also brought to the fore again the issue of the Cathedral Chaplains and their role: if the reforms pointed towards a more informal style of liturgy built around the local community, then those who had questioned their role in the solemn performance of the Divine Office might be inclined to see it as an even greater anachronism than before.

Finally, there was the question of the Cathedral music. Even those in favour of the changes admitted that there was a serious lack of good music for the vernacular services; should the Cathedral continue with the use of Latin, at least for the 'official' part of its liturgy? If it did so, there was a danger that it would cut itself off even more from the ordinary life of the diocese. Certainly there were those who wanted it to become a bastion of the traditional, holding on to the supposed beauty and mystery of the old. Others, however, believed that it should be a model to the rest of the diocese and give a lead in the implementation of the new services. Here, perhaps, the Vaughan vision was in danger of becoming a hindrance rather than an inspiration, and the very success of the 1950s made a transition difficult: the traditional had become, as it were, embedded in the very structure of the building. The pastoral liveliness of those years and Wheeler's and others' willingness to change were too easily forgotten by those traditionalists who wanted to claim the Cathedral as their own. What was needed was a new charter for a post-conciliar Cathedral.

As we have seen, Cardinal Godfrey had supported the introduction of the early liturgical changes at the Cathedral. He died in January 1963, just after the Council had completed its first session. His successor was John Carmel Heenan who, like Cardinal Godfrey, had been Archbishop of Liverpool before becoming Archbishop of Westminster. Cardinal Heenan was a much more public figure than Godfrey had ever been; he prided himself on being a priest of the people and had a strong pastoral streak – as he never forgot, he had been an active parish priest in his early years. In Liverpool he had become extremely popular with the Catholic laity, less so with the clergy who sometimes resented his quick decisiveness and his willingness to change or ignore what had become the traditional and even hallowed ways of doing things. He welcomed the liturgical changes if they seemed to have a pastoral purpose, but was less happy with the deeper theological thinking that underlay many of the Council's pronouncements; a man of unmovable certainties himself when it came to matters of faith, he found it genuinely difficult, if not impossible, to understand the wave of questioning let loose by the Council.

With regard to Cathedral matters, he had had experience in Liverpool of having to solve difficult problems. After the years of hesitation and of compromise with the original grandiose schemes bequeathed by his predecessors, he launched a competition for a modern building which could be completed in a few years and at relatively low cost. The result was a striking, modernistic cathedral ideally suited to the celebration of the new liturgy; whatever one thought of its architecture, it came alive when it had a full congregation participating in the worship of God. A problem had been solved with Heenan's usual decisiveness and speed, with due regard to both the economics and the pastoral needs of the situation. In the context of the problems awaiting him at Westminster, he was not likely to be much moved by the Vaughan vision.

Some initial continuity with the past was provided in the person of the Cathedral Administrator, Gordon Wheeler. He remained at the Cathedral until March 1964, when he left to become Coadjutor Bishop in Middlesbrough. He had been Administrator for ten years, and it had been a successful decade from several points of view. Probably he left at the right time, for it is difficult to see that he could have worked so successfully with Cardinal Heenan; in particular he did not agree with the rapidity with which the Cardinal pushed ahead with the later liturgical changes, arguing for a much longer period of preparation of the people. He was opposed to the widespread use of English in the Church's official liturgy, though he later became Chairman of the National Liturgical Commission and a member of the International Conference on English in the Liturgy and accepted the changes. He would have resisted the placing of a second altar in the sanctuary of the Cathedral to allow Mass to be said facing the people.[15] Furthermore, it was clear from early on that the Cardinal was wondering about the wisdom of keeping so many priests at the Cathedral as Chaplains to sing the Divine Office. He wrote that he felt that within two or three years no cathedral or parish church in Europe would be able to keep a large staff of priests: they would have to go 'in large numbers to missionary lands'; he doubted whether there would be enough priests left in any cathedral to do more than say Mass, hear confessions and look after the sick.[16] If that happened, what would remain of the Cathedral's role for which Wheeler and so many others had worked?

It was the new Administrator, Mgr Tomlinson, who had to plan for the introduction of English into the daily liturgy at the Cathedral. One of his concerns was to avoid too large a gap between the official liturgy, which would still be in Latin, and the other services which would have at least some English in them. He suggested that at the daily High Mass the Epistle and Gospel might be read in English from within the sanctuary and facing the people, so that the High Mass would not become a 'kind of refuge for the disgruntled'. He added that, fortunately, Evelyn Waugh disliked the High Mass even more than he disliked the use of English, so it would be unlikely that he would be among the refugees! Waugh was to complain that the Council had destroyed the beauty of the Holy Week services and that going to church had become for him a mere 'duty parade'. Other well-known writers voiced similar views – for example, Tolkien, Christopher Dawson, E. I. Watkin and Douglas Woodruff. They lamented the loss of mystery and dignity, a loss that was not balanced in their minds by the greater accessibility which the reforms gave to the majority of Catholics.[17]

The former Administrator did not give up his interest in the Cathedral and on two occasions intervened to try to stop some of the changes. It is worth looking at one of these in a little detail as it illustrates very clearly the differences between the two approaches. First of all, in 1965, the new

Administrator, Mgr Tomlinson, suggested a change to the liturgy for the Christmas Vigil service. Instead of singing the full Office of Matins in Latin before the Midnight High Mass, as had been the practice (and for which Malcolm had composed some very fine music for the responsories), Mgr Tomlinson suggested to the Cardinal that a new Vigil service be introduced, consisting of passages from Scripture read in English and responses sung by the choir; this would last about half-an-hour, less than the former service (known to the Cathedral clergy, apparently, as the 'endurance test'), and be more attractive and meaningful to the congregation. Bishop Wheeler wrote immediately to object, on his own and others' behalf. He claimed that the new Administrator had no idea of what a cathedral was meant to be, regarding it instead as a 'glorified parish church'. It had always been the great glory of Westminster, he argued, that, thanks to Vaughan's inspiration, it had carried on the complete round of the Church's worship. He believed that this 'official plenitude of prayer in the heart of government' had won for the capital the graces that the Charterhouse and the Abbey had won in earlier times. It would be the 'greatest of tragedies' if it were allowed to disappear.

The letter contains two other points of interest. Wheeler reminded the Cardinal that he had suggested a 'monastic solution' to the problem of keeping the full liturgy of the Cathedral going, but Heenan had argued that the secular clergy would never accept it – shades of Vaughan and the Benedictines so many years before! Then, in a postscript, he added a moving plea. Too many of 'our avant-garde people', he thought, underestimated the 'pastoral and converting effect of pure worship'. When he himself had first visited the Cathedral as an Anglican young man, the beauty of the High Mass and Office had had a tremendous effect even though he had not understood a word of it. Moreover, he knew that a great many converts had been started off by similar visits. The Cardinal, however, had already written to the new Administrator (from Rome, where he and Wheeler were attending the final session of the Council), to leave the decision to him; he added that he himself regarded the new service as much more suitable than the long Matins. In the event a Bible vigil was held; this included the Latin responsories, but the readings were in English; as an explanatory article put it, it would be a pity if the beautiful meditations of Christmas Matins should only be enjoyed by those able to read the Latin Breviary.[18]

Other changes were introduced in the same spirit of experimentation. A design for a movable altar which would enable the priest to face the people during Mass was submitted to the Cardinal in 1964. It was to be an aluminium structure with a wooden altar table, and was to have its own canopy to add dignity and importance to what might otherwise seem 'incidental and unremarkable'. Two years later the Cardinal was voicing his concerns about the length of the main High Mass on Sundays: he felt that it should last no more than an hour, with the sermon lasting no longer than five minutes, or seven at the very most; the singing was also taking too long, especially the plainsong graduals and tracts ('Plainsong sung by boys is lovely, but graduals sung by men are not attractive and sound even longer than they really are', he wrote), and perhaps the incensations could be reduced – perhaps the time had come to dispense with incense altogether. These suggestions were discussed by the Master of Music and the Master of Ceremonies, who promised changes to ensure a shorter Mass, including instructing the clergy not to preach for more than five minutes and introducing simple chants for the graduals; the number of incensations would be reduced but not eliminated altogether. Finally, to give the flavour of the period, in 1966 drama was allowed into the Cathedral for the first time, with the performance of a Passion play on the first three days of Holy Week: the actors were all professionals from radio and television (including one from *Coronation Street*). The Administrator tried to reassure those who in 'our poverty-stricken and puritanical days tended to be frightened at the thought of plays in church' by pointing out that we remained human when we went to church and did not become 'cardboard figures of piety'; our emotions had to be involved in what was going on. The play would, he hoped, add a new dimension to the religious life of people in the modern world.[19] Whatever may be said about the particular play, it was not a bad summary of what the reformers were trying to do.

In 1968 the Diocesan Liturgical Commission raised the general issue of experimentation in the liturgy: how far had it been officially sanctioned? How far was it desirable, and within what limits? The point was made that it would take place anyway, and so it was better to allow it to happen on a planned basis; otherwise there would just be confusion. When asked to comment, Heenan agreed that experimentation should be allowed officially to avoid 'anarchy', but it should be controlled. On the whole he did not favour experiments in parishes as it was too difficult to instruct everyone sufficiently beforehand and they could easily lead to dismay. He was quite blunt in saying that the priest who was always eager to experiment was not likely to adopt a moderate approach: 'those with the least pastoral experience are the most likely to break the hearts of their people with innovations'.[20] Given the sensitivity and caution of these remarks, it is not surprising that no major changes were introduced into the Cathedral's liturgy. Given also, however, that the years immediately after the Council saw a widespread questioning of every aspect of the Church's institutional and devotional life, it was inevitable that, sooner or later, critical attention should turn to the Cathedral. There were those who wanted a radical examination of the Cathedral *in toto* and refused to accept that the Vaughan vision was any longer relevant in a post-conciliar Church. When this questioning did take place, then reservations and criticisms were aired which may have been more widespread and longer-lived than the authorities had realized, or had cared to admit.

NOTES

1 A. Hastings, *A History of English Christianity 1920–1985* (1987), pp. 473–5. The book is an excellent detailed survey.
2 See *Catholic Directories* and *Westminster Diocesan Year Books*.
3 Rev. R. J. Wakeling, 'Urban Ministry Project' (Paper, 1978). Fr Wakeling was a Cathedral chaplain.
4 See article by Mgr Brown in *Westminster Cathedral Chronicle* (1943); and AAW, Go 2/22 (1956–57), Wheeler to Godfrey (December 1957). Vaughan's original decision to close St Mary's had led to very strong protests, some of them voiced by his long-term friend Lady Herbert of Lea, in a very outspoken letter; she claimed that the poor would never accept the Cathedral as their parish church. Her letter of 2 January 1903 survives in AAW box 'V in Bo 5'; Vaughan's reply is in Shane Leslie's edition of the correspondence, pp. 459–50.
5 AAW, Go 2/22, Godfrey to Wheeler (22 October 1957).
6 Author's interview with Fr Hollings (October 1992).
7 See *Cathedral Chronicles* for details of services; letters of Wheeler to Godfrey, AAW Go 2/22 (1958–59); author's interview with Bishop Wheeler (September 1992), and the Bishop's *In Truth and Love* (Leeds, 1990).
8 AAW, Go 2/22 (1958–59).
9 *Cathedral Chronicle* (December 1960).
10 AAW, He 3/51, Canon Guazzelli to Administrator (26 July 1964).
11 See *Cathedral Chronicle*.
12 *Cathedral Chronicle* (January 1955–February 1957).
13 Author's interview with Bishop Wheeler.
14 Hastings, p. 567.
15 Author's interview with Bishop Wheeler; Wheeler, *In Truth and Love*.
16 AAW, Box 246, Heenan to Lady Russell (18 December 1965).
17 Hastings, pp. 567–8; AAW Box 246, Tomlinson to Heenan (17 August 1964).
18 AAW, Box 246, Wheeler to Heenan (3 December 1965); Heenan to Tomlinson (27 November 1965); also *Chronicle* (December 1965).
19 AAW, Box 246, Heenan to Tomlinson (1 April 1966) and Tomlinson to Heenan (26 April 1966); *Chronicle* (March 1966).
20 AAW, Box 246, Minutes of Diocesan Liturgical Commission (23 September 1968); letter of Cardinal (6 December 1968).

Chapter 7

A time of change and crisis

IT WOULD HAVE BEEN DIFFICULT ENOUGH in the circumstances to balance tradition, principles of reform and perceived pastoral needs. Two factors intervened to make the task both harder and more pressing: one was the loss of a large number of priests through laicization in the late 1960s and 1970s, and the decline in vocations. This would have made it extremely difficult to have kept a full complement of clergy at the Cathedral, even if those in charge had been wholly convinced of the need to do so, and we have already seen Cardinal Heenan's reservations on this score. As it was, the number of Chaplains fell: in 1968 there were twenty full Chaplains and five honorary ones; by 1972 the number of full Chaplains had fallen to seventeen (having fallen to fourteen for a time in 1969), and by 1975 it was down to eleven, with seven honorary ones, and four years later it was ten, with five honorary ones; the decline continued, so that by 1988 there were only eight full Chaplains and four honorary ones.[1]

The other factor was the financial crises of the early 1970s. Such crises were nothing new in the life of the Cathedral, but the massive inflation of costs made these particular crises much worse than anything that had gone before, and made a number of people question the value of the Cathedral's contribution to the life of the diocese. Attemps had been made in the 1960s to regularize the income by two appeals to the parishioners to take part in direct giving campaigns: in 1963 Cardinal Godfrey and Gordon Wheeler introduced an offertory pledge envelope scheme, and in 1966 this was repeated by the new Cardinal and Administrator. They claimed that the first campaign had been successful in that it allowed proper budgeting to take place on the basis of a known expected income; it could now be extended to all those who used the Cathedral regularly, whether parishioners or not. What was novel about the second campaign was that it included a statement of accounts – probably the first time one had been published. Expenditure was given as £54,500 per annum, with income at £44,300 (not including income from endowments, at £4,300 for 1965). A later statement in the *Cathedral Chronicle* in 1969 made it clear that the campaign had not been as successful as had been hoped; the Cathedral needed £1,000 a week to keep going, and only in the summer months when there were plenty of visitors did anything approaching this sum come in from the Sunday and weekday offertory collections, the door money and the surplus from candle offerings.[2]

Significantly, the 1966 statement of accounts did not include a separate item for the music in the Cathedral or the Choir School – though some of the costs would have been included under the general heading of 'salaries'. 'Significantly', because the cost of the Cathedral music, including the Choir School, had always been substantial, and had been the cause of friction in the past. While the subsidy to the Choir School came from central diocesan funds and not from those collected for the Cathedral, this made little practical difference at this time of general financial stringency. As we have seen, several attempts had been made to set up an endowment fund for the music, but without success, despite the high regard and, indeed, international acclaim which the choir had won. The most recent of these attempts had been made by Wheeler in 1963, when an imaginative ecumenical scheme to endow the choirs of the Cathedral, St Paul's and the Abbey had been launched with the full support of Cardinal Heenan (as Archbishop-elect), the Archbishop of Canterbury and the Bishop of London. The aim had been to raise £500,000 and to divide this equally between the three choirs. It may have been because this appeal was still in existence that no mention of the needs of the Cathedral's music featured in the 1966 general appeal. The 'Three Choirs Appeal' had some success in setting up a Church Music Trust, but by 1968 the response was being described as 'singularly disappointing'; people were urged to support it by attending a Festival of Carols which was being put on in the Cathedral under the auspices of the Salvation Army, but in the end it failed to produce enough to enable an endowment fund to be set up. At the same time the Head of the Choir School, Fr Vincent Commerford, was writing in the Cathedral *News Sheet* (itself a sign of growing financial problems – the *Cathedral Chronicle* had proved too expensive to keep going) that the warning of the Trust that all three London choir schools might have to be closed was 'simply stating the truth' unless some additional sources of income could be found.[3]

These varied difficulties formed the background of the first attempt to work out the implications of the changes in the liturgy for the Cathedral and to draw up a new statement of its role. This happened in 1969. The Diocesan Liturgical Commission held an extraordinary meeting in the January of that year, 'to consider the part which should be played in the diocese by the Cathedral, in the light of the liturgical reforms of the Second Vatican Council'. The meeting showed that there was strong interest in a role for the Cathedral as a centre of the liturgical life of the diocese, but considerable disagreement about what that role might be. It decided that a special subcommittee should be set up to discuss the issues involved. Membership included the Benedictine Abbot of Ealing, who acted as chairman, another Benedictine priest and two laymen – one of them Colin Mawby the Master of Music, the other John East the Director of the Church Music Association – as well as the Administrator and some priests from the Cathedral.[4]

The subcommittee seems not to have had a clear idea of its brief. Some times it discussed matters which were purely administrative, at others it was concerned with the amount of English that should be allowed in the official liturgy. From the outset the Administrator took the position that the daily High Mass and Vespers must always be in Latin, only to find that at the Easter Vigil Mass the Cathedral clergy who were concelebrating insisted on doing so in English. Colin Mawby refused to agree to any proposal that would allow English to be used in any of the official services, even at Benediction, because, he said, the people had not requested such a change. The minutes of the meetings are full of his dissenting amendments and proposals, and his intransigence was clearly a trial to other members. One positive suggestion which he made was agreed to: he would try to form a 'congregational choir' for the Sunday High Mass to sing the Creed, Acclamation and *Pater noster*. Overall, very little was said about the role of the Cathedral in the diocese, and no policy document was produced.

Commenting later on the meetings, Mgr Purney, the Precentor of the Cathedral, wrote that he thought it had been a mistake to have 'outsiders' discussing the liturgy of the Cathedral, as they did not understand what it was like and what could be done, and there was a danger that they would try to use it for experiments; people might accept such experiments in their own parishes but when they came to the Cathedral they expected 'a Cathedral liturgy in the great tradition'. A similar point was made by John East: the Cathedral would lose its unique position if the capitular liturgy were ever given less respect and care than at present; it was by presenting such exemplary standards that it was a model to the parishes of the diocese – by

The Vaughan Chantry: the Cardinal was buried at Mill Hill, but an effigy
was placed in the chapel of St Thomas of Canterbury (north transept). It was
designed by John Marshall and sculpted by Henry McCarthy, who had worked
for Bentley over the years. The shield shows Vaughan's coat of arms

The Twelfth Station of the Cross, by Eric Gill. The Stations were
erected between 1914 and 1918 in the face of intense opposition

Cardinal Arthur Hinsley, Archbishop of Westminster 1935–43. The picture shows him waving from the balcony of Archbishop's House on his return from Rome as Cardinal. Photo: Daily Herald

Cardinal Bernard Griffin, Archbishop of Westminster 1943–56

Cardinal William Godfrey, Archbishop of Westminster, 1956–63

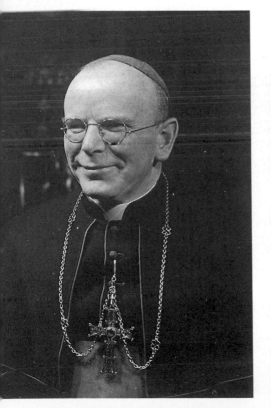

The missing pillar: Mgr Collingwood, the Administrator, had the central pillar
near the Blessed Sacrament Chapel removed because it got in the way
of processions. It was later recovered and restored. Photo: Burwoods

A family event: President
and Mrs Kennedy visited
the Cathedral in 1961 for
the christening of their
niece, Anna Christina
Radziwill. Photo:
Associated Press

being different, not by being the same. Those who spoke in this way, of the Cathedral's being a model to the rest of the diocese and of what people wanted from it, were, presumably, dismayed a few years later to find that the 'outsiders' when they were consulted had quite different and not always complimentary ideas about the Cathedral and what they wanted from it.

The Cardinal had asked Bishop Wheeler for his views. The latter replied that he felt that the bishops were in a cleft stick between the 'intransigent elderly priests who will not do anything to implement Vatican II, and the younger men who want to revolutionize everything'; the older clergy were 'blind' and of no help, while the younger ones had not got 'the humility to realise the importance of history'. He went on to claim that the realization of the Vaughan vision had been 'one of the greatest pastoral things' that had ever been done in the country. Without the official liturgy the Cathedral would very soon become a 'great white elephant', and this would be a terrible disservice to the Church throughout England 'which looks to it for inspiration'. The Bishop, however, unlike some of the other traditionalists, was quite in favour of change in line with the spirit of the age and the mind of the Church. Why not have the new Office of Readings, which had replaced Matins, held in the Blessed Sacrament chapel every evening, with just one priest leading it and with lay readers? The sung liturgy – Lauds, High Mass and Vespers – should, he believed, remain in Latin, making a 'great pastoral aurora of praise'. With regard to manpower, he acknowledged that it had always been a problem to get the right sort of priest at the Cathedral; could not an appeal be made in all the dioceses for volunteers to take on the work? He was sure that the other bishops would co-operate by releasing priests on loan for what should be 'the first and greatest of all priorities'. Here, surely, the image of the ideal was obscuring the reality.

We have Cardinal Heenan's own views, expressed informally in a letter to Mgr Bartlett, the Administrator, about the same time. He stressed the uniqueness of the Cathedral and its position in the whole country, and the acknowledged excellence of its liturgical practice – he quoted Pope Paul VI as saying that in all his travels nothing had impressed him so much as the way the liturgy was conducted at Westminster. (He had visited London in 1934 while on a private holiday to the British Isles.) The Cardinal believed that the Cathedral would never be justified in abandoning the Latin liturgy, but there was also an obligation to produce the best in the English liturgy. The morning Mass should be in Latin, but the evening Vespers in English; they had a duty not only 'to the old people who love the Latin', but also to the young people who 'quite rightly want to develop a good tradition of music to accompany the vernacular'.[5]

For Heenan the situation was becoming increasingly difficult. The divisions at the Cathedral were a weak reflection of what was happening in general in the English Catholic church, which was experiencing an increasing polarization between the conservatives and the progressives. His concern was primarily a pastoral one, to ensure that neither group were alienated to such an extent that they felt they had to leave the church. From 1964 to 1970 the radicals had published *Slant*, which was Christian Marxist in inspiration and revolutionary in word – though no more. From the mid-1960s onwards the conservatives had been forming themselves into pressure groups; there was, for example, the Catholic Priests' Association, set up in 1968 to 'combat and refute the neo-modernism which is eating at the very vitals of the church'. This was followed in 1970 by a lay movement, Pro Fide, organized by Patrick Wall, a Conservative Member of Parliament. While neither of these movements, or other similar ones, was numerically strong or likely to lead to outright schism, they represented, according to Adrian Hastings, the feelings of many traditionally-minded Catholics who felt disoriented and even betrayed by the changes in their Church, and from the authorities' point of view had to be seen in the context of Archbishop Lefebvre's very serious breakaway in Switzerland. Furthermore, the conservatives could appeal to statistics as well as to sentiment to back their case: the figures for conversions to Catholicism were showing a marked decline, from over 13,500 to 1959 to fewer than 4,000 in 1972. In the diocese of Westminster the number of people received into the Church had declined from 1,917 in 1960 to 832 in 1970 (and continued to drop, to 526 in 1980). They argued that the changes were obviously making the Church less attractive to outsiders, depriving it of both its traditional certainties and its liturgical splendour.[6]

Against this background, Heenan wanted practical solutions to tide things over until calm returned. He was becoming increasingly disillusioned by the progressives, unable as he was to feel any sympathy with their continual probing; at the same time, the conservatives were also in their own way questioning the authority of the Church and refusing to accept what seemed to him to be perfectly sensible reforms. At the Cathedral, there was a danger that the intransigence of a few would bring about the destruction of what they most wanted to preserve, by losing the sympathy of the rest of the clergy and making the building and its liturgy appear to be an expensive anachronism. At a meeting of the Westminster Senate of Priests in 1975, the

Cardinal was asked whether the demolition of the Cathedral had ever been considered – the questioner was, no doubt, just a clerical maverick, but some of his fellow priests probably shared the frustrations and the misunderstanding which lay behind the provocative question.[7]

As we have seen, the attempt in 1969 to define an up-to-date role for the Cathedral had failed. Another attempt was made in 1975. Along with the general background of uncertainty there were a number of other issues which made the discussions and a decision necessary: the future of the professional singers in the choir, doubts about the Choir School's future and the launch of another general appeal for funds which would have to have the support of the clergy of the diocese if it were to succeed. In addition to a meeting of the Senate of Priests, a special Liturgical Committee was set up for the purpose – its membership this time restricted to people who were, or who had been, directly connected with the Cathedral. It was the Senate of Priests which was most critical but it also produced some positive suggestions for reform.

The meeting was opened by the Cardinal. He pointed out that the grave financial condition of the Cathedral and said that strong feelings had been expressed that there was no need for a cathedral, and that too much money was spent on its music. He stressed, however, that it was every bit as national a church as Canterbury Cathedral was; just recently, 3,000 women from all over the country had met there, as had 3,000 Hungarians to honour Cardinal Mindszenty. What was required, he concluded, was to make it part of the diocese so that people and clergy could benefit. The speech was hardly a strong defence of a Cathedral under attack, and Colin Mawby, who had been invited to address the clergy, did little better. He referred first of all to some technical problems of the acoustics, which made it difficult for the organists and for the siting of the choir – the latter was bound to be distant from the people. Furthermore, as in the summer up to 50 per cent of the congregation was likely to be foreign visitors, there could be little feeling of community in the building.

The Master of Music then claimed that it was a red herring to think that the problem lay in the capitular liturgy; indeed, if this were allowed to remain unchanged then numbers attending the services would increase. He admitted that it was the choir's job to take part in and to express the renewal in the Church, but this must be distinct from the capitular liturgy. There was plenty to show that the Cathedral was providing a service to the diocese: there had been a summer school for the Pueri Cantores, and the choir had done much recording work and had made several appearances elsewhere, including Windsor; there were going to be two Promenade concerts later in the year, and he had formed a small orchestra and a large amateur choir which had been favourably reviewed. He would like to see special services organized in the Cathedral, and pilgrimages arranged from the parishes to it. He admitted that the atmosphere was very impersonal and that there was nothing by way of welcome; perhaps refreshments could be provided for visitors. In answer to questions about the possibility of greater participation by the people in the official liturgy, he did not see that this was possible – there were too few at the morning Mass for so large a building, and, anyway, they had a professional choir which 'should be treated professionally'. The modern hymns had not been written for a building as large as the Cathedral, and the 'traditional hymns just seemed to sound the best'. Finally, he did not see that the Cathedral had a role in guiding others in how to perform the liturgy – that had been valuable when the liturgy had been 'static' and a model could be produced for parishes to follow, but that was no longer feasible. Nor would a change of time of the principal sung Mass help; the 12.30 daily Mass was very useful for office workers, but only because it was short.

It is not surprising, after such a negative performance, that some of the clergy later called for Mawby's resignation; as one of them put it, the present Master of Music did not seem to enjoy the confidence of the clergy. They wondered whether he would ever agree to work in a new style even if one were to be established. The Cardinal clearly found it difficult to defend Mawby: while they were lucky to have such a first-class musician, he said, 'there was a great conflict of opinion'; the musicians were a very forceful body, and there were divisions among the Chaplains. At best, he thought, the Master of Music would carry out a definite order to change but it would be without any conviction.

This was being unfair to Mawby. He was stubbornly immovable on the issue of the capitular liturgy. On other aspects of the services and the music at the Cathedral, however, he had moved from his position of 1969. Earlier in 1975 he had sent a memorandum to the Cardinal with a list of practical suggestions for improving the liturgy: the choir should attend the Sunday evening Mass and sing an English Mass with full congregational participation; there should be more active participation in the 10.30 a.m. High Mass on Sundays; on one Saturday afternoon per month, instead of sung Vespers, the choir should sing a demonstration Parish Mass to which the parishes should be invited, and the Cathedral should regularly commission new English works. He had also, as he had told the Senate, widened the scope of the Cathedral's musical activities by forming amateur groups. He, and the headmaster of the Choir School, Fr Commerford, had moved a long way from the enclosed 'no concerts at any price' outlook of earlier years. Since Mawby's suggestions for change were pointing in the right direction, it is difficult to understand why he did not put them before the Senate; perhaps he sensed that some of the clergy were out to kill off the capitular liturgy, especially given the attacks on the position of the professional singers which were taking place at the same time. If the capitular liturgy were to be reduced, and the men of the choir dismissed, there would be little left to justify having a specialized choir at all.

Much of the discussion at the Senate did centre on the capitular liturgy and what, if anything, could be done to bring it up to date and allow some participation. There were, however, other issues. Questions were asked about the national role that was always claimed for the Cathedral: apart from providing a large meeting place, what else should it be doing? And if it had a national role, should not there be national support for it in terms of funding and manpower? If an appeal was about to be launched, was it for cultural, structural or religious purposes? No one seemed very clear, and yet the clergy would be asked to promote it. Finally, the issue of the appointment of the Cathedral staff was raised in a number of ways: it seemed that the administrative staff were in conflict with the liturgical staff, and that the Chaplains on the whole were not convinced of the value of what they were doing; who was responsible to whom? Were the staff even capable of implementing the necessary changes? There was, clearly, a feeling among the clergy that the Cathedral staff were remote from the rest of the diocese and that the daily performance of the capitular liturgy required a radically altered approach: it could mean nothing if it were performed by clergy without genuine conviction and by professional singers most of whom were not Catholics and may not even have been practising Christians.

At one stage in the discussions the Cardinal mentioned that at the start of his time at Westminster he had suggested that a monastic order might take on 'the prayer life of the Cathedral', but members of the secular clergy to whom he had mentioned it had been outraged. Later in the meeting, when the clergy split into working groups, one of the groups wondered whether a religious order might be 'imported for the capitular liturgy'. As we have seen, Wheeler had also at one time suggested a monastic solution. Whether this could have worked is difficult to say. Would the religious order or monks have also run the Cathedral parish, and was it this possibility that outraged the secular clergy rather than the mere performance of the capitular liturgy?

It is difficult to see any group of monks or religious being content with being rolled out each day just for a singing part. By the 1970s, anyway, it was almost certainly too late: all the monastic houses and religious orders were suffering from a decline in manpower, and were also reassessing their role in the post-conciliar world. Perhaps Vaughan had been wiser than his advisers in seeing the daily performance of the Divine Office as essentially monastic and in understanding that the English secular clergy had no cathedral tradition and would have difficulties in developing one.

It would be unfair to leave the impression that the Senate of Priests was wholly negative in its attitude to the Cathedral. There were those who saw little future for it: it was a 'mausoleum with music', it was an indication of 'our obsession with plant and buildings'. The majority, however, believed that it could have a positive role in the life of the diocese and there was general applause for the report of one of the working groups which included a range of positive suggestions as well as a criticism of the current situation. They started from the basis that people went to the Cathedral to take part in the best of the restored liturgy and to receive a welcome; the Cathedral should, therefore, be a 'shining example of Catholic liturgical life in 1975'. Whatever went on there should be 'a true Christian celebration'. Clergy should be seen 'walking about' in the building and be available for advice – this would be a useful extension of the excellent confessional service already supplied; perhaps it could also be linked to the provision of professional (lay) counselling. The use of the whole plant, and especially the Conference Hall, should be planned as a single exercise; more use should be made of the side chapels to overcome some of the problems of the size of the building. Other groups wanted a greater stress on the idea of the Cathedral as the Mother Church of the diocese: could the Cardinal or his Auxiliary Bishops appear more often at services? Could each parish take it in turn to 'adopt' the Cathedral for a week, as happened in some Anglican dioceses? The Cathedral would pray for that parish by name in its liturgy and the parish would pray for the concerns of the Cathedral and get its people to visit (and be welcomed at) the Cathedral. Finally, it was suggested that the Cathedral should become a centre of pastoral activity in every field – conferences, lectures, special preachers, cultural events, more services for diocesan groups, and so on. Allowing for the changes of the post-conciliar age we are not far in all this from what Vaughan had said he had always wanted – a 'live' Cathedral.

There is nothing that is revolutionary in these suggestions: indeed, they may appear surprisingly non-radical, given the amount of criticism which had been voiced. While the clergy wanted a Cathedral with a mission for the world of the 1970s they did not think that that involved a complete upheaval; much could be achieved by a change of attitude in those in charge and by a willingness to give up the idea that the capitular liturgy was untouchable. If they could be said to have had a simple aim it was probably the fuller integration of the Cathedral into the life of the diocese.

What of the 'insiders'? The Special Liturgical Committee met later in the same year, and it says a great deal for the skill of the Administrator, Mgr Bartlett, that he was able to move the members towards change. He told the Cardinal that he had found the discussions 'impossibly difficult', but he finally got agreement for a sung English Mass with the choir on Sundays at 5.30 p.m. – Mawby agreed to this, as he had already suggested it, but made it plain that he still could not accept any change in the capitular liturgy with 'interest or enthusiasm'. At one point in the discussions it had been suggested that the Master of Music might himself write some music for the Mass in English; this, according to the minutes, was met with 'somewhat less than much enthusiasm'! The committee also agreed (by six votes to one) that the Morning Prayer before the 10.30 a.m. High Mass on Sundays should be in English, and that the congregation should be encouraged to participate through the use of a printed edition of the Psalms, to be prepared by the Cathedral. Finally, there was unanimous agreement that the staffing of the Cathedral with adequate numbers and able priests was of paramount importance, even though they were all aware of the lack of priests and of interest in the Cathedral which the Vicar General claimed he was finding in the diocese.

There was still no new charter or mission statement to take the Cathedral forward into the 1980s and beyond. But at least the need for change was generally acknowledged. Perhaps the best statement of the new outlook was contained in a memorandum for discussion drawn up by Fr Andrew Morley, one of the Chaplains, and presented to the Committee at its final meeting. After listing a number of practical suggestions he ended with the following:

in general, an enthusiastic and persevering effort should be maintained to revitalize the sung liturgy at the Cathedral, with a particular emphasis on its pastoral nature. With such a real effort it must be possible in a relatively short time to remodel present attitudes and practice, so that they would conform to the reformed liturgy. Present problems should be capable of solution by providing a house of prayer which would blend the solemnity and professionalism expected of a Cathedral church on special occasions, with a more flexible, simple and yet moving and beautiful celebration which would have the sole purpose of leading the people in prayer and which would also be worthy of emulation by others.

All the discussions in 1975 took place against the background of another major financial crisis.[8] To resolve this, and put the finances of the Cathedral on a more stable foundation for the longer term, a major new appeal was planned which would be professionally launched and managed. A previous appeal had been closed in June 1973, having reached only a fifth of its target; it had been advertised specifically as having no connections with professional fund-raisers. Because of the crisis the Cathedral authorities had to deal with a question which had been implicit in the discussions about the liturgy and the role of the Cathedral in the diocese: the future of the professional singers in the choir and the existence of the Choir School. To understand the seriousness of the situation it is necessary to say something about the Cathedral finances.

In the mid-1950s, an annual account of receipts and expenditure expressed in percentages would have looked something like this:

Receipts	Income from dividends, reserves and endowments	29%
	Voluntary offerings (door and offertory)	37%
	Sales/visitors (e.g. tower, candles, postcards)	22%
	Donations	5%
	Sundries	7%
Expenditure	Repairs, maintenance, ongoing work	24%
	Salaries (esp. choirmen, clergy, sacristans)	30%
	Archbishop and clergy households	23%
	Altar costs	4%
	Printing, advertising, postcards	4%
	Thanksgiving fund	3%
	Sundries (incl. lighting)	12%

The receipts balanced the expenditure of about £50,000 each year, and sometimes there was a very small surplus to carry forward.[9] Not included in these accounts was the annual subsidy to the Choir School (about £8,000), which came from general diocesan funds, nor the costs of any extensive work on the decoration of the Cathedral, as this was only done when funds were available from special donations, appeals or bequests. For example, Cardinal Griffin had established the 'Million Crown Fund' appeal;

according to this a person became a Friend of Westminster Cathedral by collecting ten crowns (50 shillings) over a period of time, the money to go towards the completion of the fabric and its decoration. Clearly, in these years the Cathedral was in a comparatively healthy position, although it appears that the reserves were being called on relatively heavily. Any major increase in expenditure, for example for repairs, would cause problems. We have seen already that attempts were made in 1963 and 1966 to increase the income from voluntary offerings by launching 'direct giving' campaigns.

It is not possible to compare the public accounts which were issued in 1966 for the first time with the ones used for the tables above as they were drawn up in a different way and in less detail. Three points may be made, however: the amount paid out in salaries had risen to about 38 per cent of the total expenditure; the amount spent on repairs had dropped to 10 per cent, while the amount coming in from offertory and door collections had jumped from just over £17,000 in the 1950s to £34,000 in 1965. This last figure is all the more impressive since at the time of the 1963 'direct giving' appeal the weekday collections had been stopped altogether. It appears that the Cathedral was just managing to balance its books in the mid-1960s, perhaps this time with a small annual deficit.

By 1970 one particular item was calling for urgent action, and that was Cathedral maintenance. The long-term consultant architect for the Cathedral, Laurence Shattock, submitted a report on the fabric which drew attention to the need for certain repairs, especially to the roofs. These had been damaged during the war and the repairs done afterwards had patched them up without doing a thorough job. Shattock argued that if the repairs were not done soon, serious damage would result. He had, he said, been reporting this for some years, but had always been urged by the Administrator, Mgr Bartlett, to keep maintenance costs to the minimum and so the work had not been done. He estimated that a sum of £20,000 needed to be spent straight away. This was not done, and three years later he reported that he deeply regretted that so much that needed to be done to maintain 'this beautiful building in an appropriate condition' had to be left undone because of financial difficulties.[10]

The inflation of the early 1970s had the same effects on the Cathedral as elsewhere: it increased costs, especially wages, without bringing a comparable increase in income. By 1973 it was necessary to have a look at the whole financial position of the Cathedral, especially as the appeal had failed. A report of that year projected a cumulative deficit of £24,500 for the year, rising to £52,700 in 1974 and a huge £84,100 in 1975. It also estimated that the cost of the choir would rise from the £11,500 of 1970 to £15,000 in 1975, and this did not include the subsidy to the Choir School from diocesan funds of over £9,000 in 1970 rising to an estimated £14,700 in 1975. Clearly, substantial economies would have to be made; if some of the diocesan clergy were unhappy about the liturgical value of the choir and the music at the Cathedral, then these figures would convince them that some of the savings could be made in that area. This is the background to what may be called the great music crisis of 1975.[11]

From Terry's time onwards the Masters of Music had regarded the professional singers of the choir as its backbone, especially given the particular stress that there had been on early polyphonic music. Almost from the beginning, there had been attempts to reduce their number and importance, and we have seen that it had been one of Terry's complaints that his 'singing men' had not remained at full strength. The most recent attacks had come in 1970, this time on financial grounds; it was felt by the Administrator that a sum between £5,000 and £7,000 was the maximum that could be afforded, instead of the £10,000 or so that the choir was costing. One suggestion was that Colin Mawby should be retained and given an annual sum of £5,000 to spend as he thought best. Later, in 1971, Mgr Bartlett thought that the moving of the Choir School to Hitchin (while repairs and alterations were done to its buildings) would provide an excellent opportunity to get rid of the professional singers altogether, as there would be no weekly choral performances in the Cathedral while the boys were away. This would be the situation from January 1972, and so the men could be given plenty of notice. A sum of £1,500 could be provided (in addition to Mawby's own salary and that of a professional organist) to hire singers on an occasional basis for special functions. If this happened, then Mawby would be forced to replan the choral part of the Cathedral's liturgy – 'creatively', Bartlett added optimistically.[12]

The opportunity was not taken, apparently because the Cardinal stepped in to save the choir. Salaries for the choir came to £11,400 in 1972, and the figure rose to £13,800 in 1973. In the following year the men claimed an 18 per cent pay rise, and while this was not thought to be unreasonable it could not be met, and so in December 1974, the men were given three months' notice of possible dismissal.[13]

There was an immediate outcry in the national press. A number of leading musicians, including André Previn, Lennox Berkeley and Yehudi Menuhin, wrote to *The Times* to condemn the Cathedral authorities. Writers to *The Daily Telegraph* and *The Guardian* stressed that the comparatively small sum of money required must be found – Mawby himself had written to *The Times* to say that only £20,000 would be needed over two years to keep the choir in existence until the national appeal began to bring in money. An editorial in *The Tablet* argued for diocesan and national funding for the Cathedral and its liturgy, but also argued that changes should be made in that liturgy to make it more acceptable to a modern congregation. It refused to take sides in the present dispute, however, until there was 'public accounting' – how else could people know whether the upkeep of the choir really was so costly that it could not be afforded? This last point is interesting in the light of an article in the magazine of the Society of St Gregory, *Music and Liturgy*. This made a strong attack on the Council of Administration of the Cathedral, which had taken the decision in the first place. According to the article, the council had acted hastily and in secret without proper consultation; the Cardinal was absent because of illness, and there was, anyway, no shortage of money because of recent successful property deals. *The Tablet*'s call for the publication of accounts was surely justified if a reputable magazine could claim that the Cathedral had 'plenty' of money in the very year that it was heading for a cumulative deficit of nearly £100,000.

The issue of money was raised again in an article in *Music and Musicians* in March 1975. It asked why so much had been spent on rebuilding the Choir School so recently if the 'effective functioning of the choir' was to be thwarted – the article claimed that £100,000 had been spent, of which the diocese had provided £30,000. It also carried on the attack on the Cathedral authorities by accusing them of the sort of insensitive behaviour common to those whose job is just to administer. In support, it dragged up the case of Graham Greene, who had been asked to remove parts of his novel *The Power and the Glory*, and that of the Eric Gill altarpiece which had been 'butchered'. In such ways, it argued, 'seemingly good intentions have been signs of an uncultured and iconoclastic mentality': to destroy the beauty of the Cathedral's music and its outstanding international reputation for a relatively small sum of money would be unforgivable. The attack was plainly unfair, and there was no easy money available. Early in 1975 Mawby made appeals to Hugh Jenkins, the Minister for the Arts, and to the Arts Council, without any success. In the end, just before the notice of dismissal expired, a grant of £8,000 was received from the Music Trust, and this was used to keep the professional singers in the choir for another year.

The issue had raised some telling points. There had been a lack of overall policy-making at the Cathedral for some years, and it seemed to need a crisis to get those in charge to think very far beyond the day-to-day administration.

The failure to reform the liturgy and the music in 1969 and to produce a new 'charter' had been due in large part to an unwillingness to deal with vested, traditional interests and to sort out the divisions within the Cathedral staff. A new national appeal was being planned during this crisis over the music; how much would people be told of the true state of the Cathedral's finances, and how much would the apparent lack of a sharp focus for the appeal make it less successful? We have seen that Colin Mawby had made concessions over the liturgy and had offered ways in which diocese and Cathedral could become more integrated, and he had won a reprieve for his professional singers. He was mistaken, however, to claim in an article in *The Times* (April 1975) that the 'victory' demonstrated 'the affection which ordinary people had for the traditional cathedral music'. The whole article, indeed, had a note of triumph which could not have inspired much confidence that further, genuine reform would be forthcoming: the 'contemporary myth put about by some fashionable, shallow thinkers that cathedrals were obsolete' had been destroyed, it was claimed, and the 'narrow thinking accountants' had been put firmly in their place. The Master of Music might argue that 'Art' must have a high financial priority, and that the Church must 'defend and extend its cultural activity', but the accountants were not to be that easily defeated nor the clergy that readily won over.

One of the arguments used by those who wished to get rid of the professional singers was that the music for the liturgy could be performed by the excellent boys choir trained in the Cathedral Choir School. Part of Mawby's reason for trying so hard to hang on to the men was that he could see that without the men the boys could not perform the type of music which had become the staple of the Cathedral's official liturgy. Furthermore, if the men were allowed to go, there could be a strong case for getting rid of the boys as well and relying on a lay amateur choir. After all, the Choir School was even more expensive than the men singers, although its subsidy came from the general diocesan fund and not directly from the Cathedral. As the diocese was heading for a deficit of about one million pounds by 1975 it was not surprising that Mawby's philistine accountants looked at the Choir School to see if its costs could be reduced or even eliminated.

Any attempt, however, to close the school or to alter it radically would inevitably bring the authorities into conflict with the boys' parents. An additional complication from the authorities' point of view was that a long period of notice of even possible closure would have to be given, to enable the parents and staff to make alternative arrangements. Those who were opposed to such a move would then have ample time to launch a public campaign against it. This is what happened in 1975 when the Cardinal agreed that notice should be given to the parents that the Choir School might have to close with effect from summer 1976. A meeting was held in October of parents, school staff, Governors, Colin Mawby and members of the choir, and representatives of the Cathedral Parish Council, the Diocesan Council of Administration and of the Appeals Committee. The meeting had been arranged at the request of the parents following the receipt of a letter from Fr Commerford, the headmaster, about the possible closure. The Cardinal was too ill to attend but he sent a letter which Canon Longstaff (secretary of the Council of Administration) read out.[14]

The Cardinal started by assuring the parents that he regarded the Choir School as unique and so would do all he could to ensure its continued existence. If the coming appeal were successful then the school could be kept open, 'unless inflation gets completely out of hand'. The appeal, he went on, was both for the maintenance of the Cathedral and for its music, and that included both the men and the boys. Canon Longstaff then got down to business, after pointing out that the parents' involvement could only extend to the financial aspects of the issue and could 'in no way extend into any political aspects there may be'. What did he have in mind? Perhaps it was no more than a restatement of the traditional role of the laity as providers of finance; they were not being consulted about the place of music in the life of the Cathedral or about the desirability of remodelling its liturgy and the effect this might have on the Choir School.

The financial figures given by Canon Longstaff needed little comment. Whereas in the early days the school had been staffed by priests and nuns whose remuneration had been minimal, it was now staffed almost entirely by lay people who had to be paid proper salaries. This, and the recent escalation of costs because of inflation, was the reason for the massive increase in the subsidy which the diocese had had to provide. This had risen from £800 in 1964/5 to £6,000 in 1968/9 and to £10,000 in 1969/70. By 1973/4 it had risen further, to £17,420 and in the past financial year (1974/5) it had been £22,660; the estimate for 1975/6 was for a further rise, to £25,700. The estimates did not take account of any further rises in inflation. He continued by saying that the question was whether a sum of at least £26,000 could be found each year, as the diocese no longer had the means to continue the subsidy. He outlined two possibilities. First of all, the fees could be raised again, from £456 to £1,121 for Probationers and from £399 to £1,066 for Choristers; such increases would, however, put the fees beyond the means of the parents. Secondly, a sum could be raised for investment – say,

£300,000, although even this would not cover improvements and repairs, just as the annual subsidy had not covered the 'enormous sum' recently spent by the diocese on the school buildings. Such a sum might come from the appeal. The Canon stressed, however, that the Cathedral itself would make heavy calls on any money raised; the structure was letting in water, there was not enough money to employ an adequate number of vergers, and the heating and lighting costs had 'increased beyond all belief'. An investment fund was needed to cover running costs, to provide for the clergy, to ensure adequate insurance cover, and so on. The appeal was aiming to raise £500,000, but it was hoped that this would be exceeded; it would have three specified objectives: immediate repairs, long-term maintenance and the Cathedral music. It would be up to the Cardinal to decide how the proceeds would be divided between these.

From the parents' point of view it was not feasible to wait for the result of the appeal – this was only going to be launched in March of the following year, by which time any decision relating to a September intake of pupils would have had to be taken. Some suggestions were made at the meeting: a separate appeal just for the school might be launched, but it would almost certainly be fishing in the same pool as the general appeal; people could be invited to become Friends of the Choir School and to contribute a regular sum each year; the fees might be raised, as they were still below those of other preparatory schools in London. Interestingly, no mention was made of the possibility of increasing the number of boys at the school – there were only 39 boys there at the time, and even a modest increase would have brought in more money and gained some economies of size. Perhaps there was a fear that the ethos of the school would suffer and its good academic record be put at risk with larger numbers. In the end it was agreed that the parents should approach the Cardinal with a plan for a stay of execution which would allow the early success of the appeal to be gauged: they would make every effort to raise about £25,000 themselves to cover the loss of the subsidy from the diocese and to ensure the school's existence for at least another year.

In a letter to the Cardinal after the meeting the Chairman of the Parents' Committee requested his permission for them 'to work on public relations between the Choir School and the clergy'. There was a feeling, she went on, that the Cathedral and the Choir School were insular and that the musical and liturgical interests of both were very narrow, so that those who paid for their upkeep felt that they got little back in return. If better relations could be established with the clergy then the work of securing the School's future could be carried out in an atmosphere of 'interest and understanding, rather than disinterest and even antagonism'. Were the parents, after all, getting involved in the politics of the situation?

Cardinal Heenan died in the November of the same year, only a week or so after he had met the Parents' Committee. His death was unexpected, although he had been in bad health for some time. In September he had made plans for his retirement. This last crisis set him thinking again about the solution which he had had in mind at the beginning of his years at Westminster – the use of a monastic choir to perform the daily Office. Shortly before he died he wrote that his clerical advisers had stressed that the diocesan clergy would not accept such a solution; in the light of what was happening he was now sorry that he had listened to their advice. The monastery which he had approached had been Ampleforth.[15] In the event the school was not closed, and the Diocesan Council of Administration agreed in December 1975 to carry any deficit incurred until July 1977. This would give the parents time, it was hoped, to launch their own appeal properly; to date they had raised £6,500 but reckoned that an annual income of £30,000 would be needed in addition to the fee income.[16]

Given the insistence of the problems which were affecting the Cathedral it is not surprising that the months before the appointment of a new Archbishop should have been used for a sort of stock-taking by writers in the Catholic press. *The Tablet* linked the imminent appointment with the opening up of the building through the new piazza to offer some reflections on the future of the Cathedral. Its great spiritual, liturgical and musical traditions were at risk because of the financial crisis – the building could not even be heated properly any longer. Perhaps it was time, the writer suggested, for the whole of the financial and domestic management of the Cathedral to be handed over to lay people, to free the clergy for their spiritual duties. There seemed to be a reluctance, the article continued, to learn from the experience of the Anglican cathedrals – why was there no group of Friends of Westminster Cathedral? Why did visitors go to St Paul's or the Abbey or Notre Dame in Paris by the coachload, but not to the Cathedral? Why were there not stronger links with parishes throughout the diocese, with parishes adopting a particular chapel or creating other special links? Why was it so difficult to find out information about what was going on – who the priests were, who was preaching, what music would be performed? The overall impression, the writer thought, was of an 'inward-looking community, hardworking, devoted but impersonal, unaware of the needs of the hungry sheep'. Finally, the article touched on an issue which was being raised up and down the country in many Catholic parishes: why were the faithful always being asked for money but never being allowed to see proper financial accounts?; why should they contribute blindly?[17]

The appointment of Basil Hume, Abbot of Ampleforth, to succeed Cardinal Heenan was announced in February 1976. *The Tablet* used this occasion to be more positive about the Cathedral. It was, it claimed, a sign of a welcome other-worldliness, an 'instinctive manifestation of faith', a challenge to a purely utilitarian outlook; along with all the cathedrals in the country, Catholic and Anglican, it needed to be preserved, not as a work of art but as 'great reservoir of prayer' and a place for contemplation. The coming of the new Archbishop coincided with the launching of a new financial appeal on a scale not previously seen: the list of patrons included the Archbishop of Canterbury and the Moderator of the General Assembly of the United Reformed Church; leading political figures; Lennox Berkeley, Colin Davis, Benjamin Britten, Ralph Richardson and Alec Guinness from the arts world, and many others. As the writer pointed out, it was unprecedented that the Duke of Edinburgh should have agreed to attend the opening concert and that another royal, the Duke of Gloucester, should have become a member of an architectural subcommittee. The aim of the appeal was to raise one million pounds, half of it to go towards the repair and maintenance of the fabric, and half towards the upkeep of the choir and music and the 'cost of making the Cathedral available for many new purposes in its renewed life'; the work on the fabric was 'the essential background' for a renewal 'of the whole spirit of the place'. In another article in the same issue Cardinal Heenan's former secretary argued that the Cathedral had a 'great and apostolic role' to play in the life of the diocese – what was needed was a firm policy and imaginative leadership.[18] In this respect, much was expected from the new Archbishop: to some extent he was an outsider able to bring a fresh outlook to the Cathedral and its problems. At the same time his monastic background would, it was hoped, ensure a sympathy with its fundamental role of being a living house of prayer through the daily recital of the Church's Divine Office.

NOTES

1   See *Westminster Diocesan Year Books* for details.
2   AAW, Go 2/22 (1962–63), 1963 Appeal Brochure; Box 246, Westminster Cathedral Administrator, 1966 Direct Giving Plan; *Cathedral Chronicle* (1969).
3   AAW, Go 2/22 (1962–63), Wheeler to Heenan (11 September 1963); Cathedral *News Sheet* (August and December 1968).

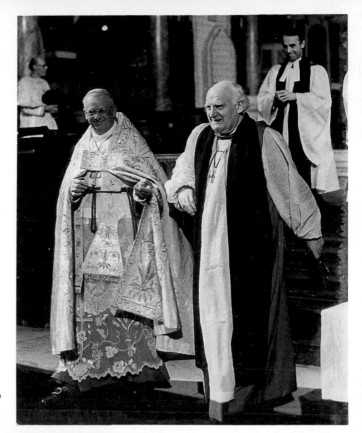

Westminster and Canterbury:
Cardinal Heenan and Archbishop
Ramsey on the latter's official visit to
the Cathedral in 1968. Photo:
Keystone Press Agency

Cardinal John Carmel Heenan,
Archbishop of Westminster
1963–75, seen here arriving
at the Cathedral for his installation as
Archbishop. Photo: Press Association

The Piazza, opened in 1975. Photo: Central Press Photos

The visit of Pope John Paul II in 1982: the English and Welsh bishops line up
to greet the Pope as he arrives outside the Cathedral. Photo: Press Association

The Papal High Mass in the Cathedral. Photo: Press Association

The spiritual centre of the diocese: At the Chrism Mass in Holy Week the Cardinal
concelebrates with his clergy and blesses the holy oils to be used throughout the diocese

4 AAW, Box 198, Cathedral Choir School, Folder 1974–75; this contains earlier minutes and memoranda as background.
5 AAW, Box 198, letters between Wheeler and Heenan (June and July 1969) and Heenan to F. Bartlett (November 1969).
6 A. Hastings, *A History of English Christianity 1920–1985* (1987) pp. 636–9; also *Westminster Diocesan Year Books*.
7 See note 4 above. The following pages are based on these documents.
8 AAW, Box 46, Westminster Cathedral Administrator, Folder 1972–74.
9 AAW, 1954 Westminster Cathedral Parish accounts.
10 See note 8 above.
11 Ibid., Westminster Cathedral Report and Budget 1973.
12 AAW, Box 198, letters of Bartlett to Heenan (November 1970 to April 1971).
13 Ibid., Cathedral Choir School Folder 1974–75.
14 Ibid.
15 Ibid., Heenan to Lady Russell (18 December 1965).
16 Report in *The Tablet* (6 December 1975), p. 1205.
17 *The Tablet* (3 January 1976), p. 17.
18 *The Tablet* (28 February 1976), pp. 205–6.

Chapter 8

The Cathedral in the modern age

IN 1979 a future Administrator of the Cathedral, recently appointed as a Chaplain, summed up his early impressions of working there and of what changes might be needed to develop its mission. The Cathedral, he wrote, had its 'glories' – the music, the range of services, the pastoral work (especially in the confessional), and on those foundations the future had to be built. There was bound to be, he continued, a tension between the present and the past in any church which was trying to reach contemporary people with a perennial message: while 'savouring the riches of the past, the Cathedral must be in the forefront of renewal'. It would have to offer new approaches in the liturgy in order to make the most of the use of English in the language of worship and its music; it would have to bring 'modern biblical and theological insights to bear on devotional piety', experiment with new-style devotions, and give a lead in the introduction of new penitential and counselling services, while 'embracing ecumenism with relish'.[1] To introduce the new while consolidating the tried and tested would extend still further the balancing skills needed by the Cathedral authorities. While much had been achieved during Cardinal Heenan's time, it had been overshadowed by the problems of his later years. As we have seen, much was hoped for from the new Cardinal.

We may look, first of all, at what happened in respect of the Choir School and the Cathedral Choir. If these had gone, as had seemed likely at one time, it would not just have ended a musical tradition of outstanding excellence. Something integral to the Cathedral as it had developed from the days of Vaughan onwards would have gone with it. Fortunately, the Choir School was kept going in the hope that the appeal of 1976 would be successful; it was, and, with a subsidiary 'Voice of Westminster Cathedral' appeal in 1982, the School was secure. By 1985, the headmaster could report that the targets had been reached, and that £300,000 would be invested to provide the funds required to enable the school to take choristers in at reduced fees; a further £100,000 would be used to provide additional financial assistance to families who needed it (completely free places are available in some circumstances). Another £100,000 would be set aside for the provision of extra accommodation (especially music rooms) for the school. The parents had lived up to their promises at the time of the crisis in the 1970s and had raised almost £70,000 on their own. No wonder a special musical evening was held in the Cathedral on the Feast of the Annunciation that year, in the presence of the Cardinal and the Duchess of Kent, with the Master of Music giving a recital on the restored great organ and the boys singing Holst's *Ave Maria* as a hymn of thanks.[2]

This assurance of a brighter future was not just because the finances of the school had been put on a sounder footing. The Cardinal had introduced a number of major changes, drawing, no doubt, on his experience in the school at Ampleforth. In 1977 a new headmaster was appointed, a layman, Peter Hannigan. The decision was taken to expand the school by admitting day boys who would be distinct from the boarding choristers in not having anything to do with the liturgy of the Cathedral. This increased the numbers at the school to ninety, a much more viable number educationally and economically – the day boys paid full fees as they would have done at any other London preparatory school. Of the ninety boys, approximately sixty are currently day boys, paying full fees, while the thirty choristers pay approximately half fees. If the Choir School was to be successful in attracting day pupils, then it had to be able to offer an academic education that would enable the boys to sit the Common Entrance examination and move on to the schools of their choice after their four or five years there; much had been done to build up a reputation for academic success in the 1960s, and this has been continued – the choristers almost all get music scholarships, the day boys go on to Ampleforth, Downside, Westminster, Eton, St Paul's, Harrow and elsewhere. The school is currently listed as providing an outstanding musical training, and teaching which is 'imaginative and at times inspired'.[3]

The staff are now entirely lay, and half of the highly qualified teachers are female. The atmosphere and regime in the school have, of course, changed; there is more of a family atmosphere, a more kindly feel to the place than would have been noticeable thirty years ago; here the school is only reflecting the changes which have affected preparatory schools in general. But its purpose is as serious as ever: the school aims, in the words of Peter Hannigan, 'to provide choristers to sing to the glory of God in the Cathedral, and to train boys, choristers and non-choristers alike, who, when they grow up, will make a vital contribution both to the music of the Church and the life of their parishes'.[4]

The choristers sing in the Cathedral seven days a week. The changes in the Divine Office have reduced their contribution, however, and on weekdays they now only sing at the solemn sung Mass at 5.30 p.m. (Vespers are sung at 5 p.m. by the men of the choir). On Sundays and major feast-days they will also sing solemn Vespers and Benediction in the afternoon. Any reduction here has been more than balanced by a huge increase in the extra-Cathedral work of the choir – concerts, broadcasts, visits and tours to other countries, and recordings. In 1986 the choir visited the United States, in 1987 they sang in Rome at the beatification of the British martyrs, in 1992 they sang in Spain at Expo '92, made a tour of south-western France and then teamed up with the choir of St Paul's Cathedral to sing in Notre Dame, Paris. They performed at the Proms in 1991, 1992 and 1993; in 1991 they sang a programme of Spanish liturgical music from the sixteenth century. This type of polyphonic music continues to be the staple of their provision, as it was in Terry's day, and they have won high critical acclaim for their singing of it at various festivals – one national critic in 1990 called them 'without doubt the best cathedral choir in the country at present'.[5] But their recordings show that they have widened their repertoire considerably, and their recent series has included Stravinsky as well as Palestrina, along with more nineteenth-century works and recordings of Mexican and Portuguese church music.

While praise for the Choir School improvements must go to Peter Hannigan, it would be unjust to forget the work done in very difficult circumstances by his predecessor, Fr Vincent Commerford. He had been appointed Vice-Rector of the School in 1962 and its Rector in 1966, and had remained in charge during the difficult post-Vatican II days and the severe financial crises of the early 1970s. The school had been largely rebuilt in 1972; academic standards had continued to rise, and he had overseen the introduction of lay staff after the departure of the Sisters. There had been a welcome widening of activities after the almost monastic dedication to the capitular liturgy under Wheeler and Malcolm. A visit to Rome in 1970 to sing at the canonization of the English martyrs had been a highlight; the choir had replaced the official Vatican choir for the occasion, and the official report had spoken of the 'perfect balance' between plainsong and polyphony that had been achieved and of the 'graceful harmony' between choir and congregation.[6] There were recordings for the BBC, and co-operation between the choir and two new groups established by the Master of Music, Colin Mawby – a Cathedral string orchestra, and an amateur choral society known as the New Westminster Chorus. On Easter Sunday 1973, all three combined to perform Mozart's Coronation Mass as the main sung Mass. It was a pity that these developments came at a time of crisis which threatened the continuance of the Choir School, but while the school may have been near to closure, that was not a reflection on the quality of the work being done. All the potential was there for further development in more favourable conditions.

The development of the Choir has been due to the Masters of Music who have built on the post-war work of George Malcolm and Colin Mawby. These have been Stephen Cleobury, David Hill and, currently, James O'Donnell. The appointment of the first two of these broke with tradition in that they were not Catholics. The importance of this lay in the fact that they brought in to the singing of the Cathedral choir something of the Anglican tradition which was their background (as, indeed, it is of the current Master of Music, James O'Donnell, a Catholic). This has resulted in a fruitful cross-fertilization of styles, and in some toning down of the very forthright sound which Malcolm had created and which was usually seen to be Continental rather than English. But O'Donnell believes that the style is still recognizably from the Malcolm tradition – a resonant, committed and even passionate sound, well-suited to the clear projection of polyphonic music in a building as large as the Cathedral, and frequently praised by the critics.[7] With regard to the choir's repertoire of music for the Cathedral services, it is still dominated by polyphony and plainsong. This is not due to a failure to be varied and adventurous, but reflects the basic task of the choir to provide music which serves the needs of the liturgy, enhancing it and adding to its prayerful character without being obtrusive or becoming a performance in its own right.

After the uncertainties and experiments of the 1970s, the weekly liturgy celebrated in the Cathedral settled down. The reduced capitular liturgy consisted on weekdays of solemn Mass sung at 5.30 p.m., preceded by Vespers at 5 p.m. – on Tuesdays these were sung in English. Morning Prayer was said at 7.40 a.m.; on Saturdays the Mass was sung at 10.30 a.m., with Evening Prayer at 5.30 p.m. On Sundays the solemn Mass was at 10.30 a.m., preceded by Morning Prayer at 10 a.m.; solemn Vespers and Benediction were sung at 3.30 p.m. On Sundays there were also six other public Masses, starting at 7 a.m. On Mondays to Fridays there were seven other Masses, including one said in Latin and two around midday. Something has already been said about Confessions; these were heard from 11 a.m. to 6 p.m. on Mondays to Fridays, from 9 a.m. to 7 p.m. on Saturdays and for nine hours on Sundays. A development here was the provision of facilities to allow for the extension of the traditional penitential role to include a modern counselling one.

There were other services too, of course: the Rosary was usually recited after the evening Mass on Mondays to Fridays; Benediction was held during a Holy Hour on Monday evening, and with the Rosary and Litany of Our Lady after Mass on Saturday evening. A prayer group met every Monday, and the Guild of the Blessed Sacrament also met on Mondays. There were special youth Masses, and a folk choir sang the 5.30 evening Mass on the first and third Sundays of each month. To show how the musical tradition was being broadened mention might also be made of the Challoner Choir which sang at the evening Mass on the first Saturday of each month; this consisted of people from the parishes in the diocese, and the aim was to give as many people as possible an opportunity to sing in the Cathedral and to 'enrich its life by welcoming new friends from the diocese'; there are echoes here of some of the earlier suggestions about ways of helping the Cathedral to develop a higher profile in the parishes. It was hoped that a regular core of singers would emerge who could contribute to the liturgy on other occasions as well. The Saturday evening Mass was often the occasion for a visiting choir to perform in the Cathedral: over a period of three months in 1993, for example, the singing was done by the Cardinal Vaughan School Choir, the Challoner Choir, the Nicholson Singers, Beckenham Parish Choir and the Whitton Choir.[8]

It is very difficult to obtain accurate statistics relating to the number of people who use the Cathedral and its services. Parishes have to make an annual return of certain figures, and these are normally published in the *Year Book*. The Mass attendance figures are for a single Sunday in the year, usually in October; the other figures published are for infant baptisms, converts received and marriages solemnized. The following table shows the figures for the Cathedral:

	1970	1980	1990
Sunday Mass attendance	2,095	3,600	3,987
Infant baptisms	122	70	122
Converts	21	15	21
Marriages	77	55	42

Not many conclusions can be drawn safely from these figures. The number of people using the Cathedral for Sunday Mass has risen markedly, while over the same period total Mass attendances in the diocese have dropped by 29 per cent. The number of converts has returned to its 1970 level, after a noticeable dip in the 1970s when only nine people were received in 1977, compared with an overall diocesan drop of 22 per cent. Again, after a sharp dip in the late 1970s the number of infant baptisms has returned to its 1970 level (the diocesan figure has dropped by 31 per cent), while the number of marriages celebrated in the Cathedral has dropped by 45 per cent compared with a diocesan drop of 22 per cent. Across the country as a whole, the worst years for Catholic losses had been from the mid-1960s to the early or mid-1970s, the decade immediately after the Second Vatican Council. By the early 1990s the Cathedral was at least holding its own and the changes in its liturgy and general provision were proving attractive.[9]

The outstanding event to take place in the Cathedral in this period was the papal visit. It was a purely pastoral visit, of course, but that it did take place, given the outbreak of the Falklands War, was due to the careful diplomacy of the Cardinal. Pope John Paul II arrived in England on Friday 28 May 1982, and on the same day said his first Mass in the country at Westminster Cathedral; he concelebrated with all the English bishops and four visiting Cardinals, in the presence of Anglican, Free Church and Orthodox representatives. It was an impressive and exciting occasion. For his sermon he took the theme of baptism, stressing the unity which it should bring about among Christians. He referred to the Cathedral, as a 'symbol of the faith and energy of the English Catholic community', while its style of architecture, unusual in England, brought to mind other parts of the Christian world and so was a reminder of the universality of the Church. The occasion is marked by a marble tablet (presented by the Friends of the Cathedral in 1984) set into the floor of the nave just in front of the sanctuary; the Latin inscription may be translated as 'Here is the place where the Supreme Pastor, John Paul II, as a pilgrim in England celebrated his first Mass on the 28th day of May, 1982. May God be glorified in everything.' In the evening the Pope returned to Archbishop's House to dine with the English bishops. He spoke to them formally about their ministry, and about the collegiality which allowed local churches to contribute to the universal Church. He also spoke about the laity and how the increased scope of the lay apostolate was so important: by fulfilling their own role they 'offer a great service of loving support to their pastors'.[10]

In his farewell address at Cardiff airport, Cardinal Hume said that one of the things which the Pope had done during his visit was to encourage the laity to take a full and active part in the Church (which implied more than 'loving support', perhaps). Coming as it did so shortly after the great National Pastoral Congress in Liverpool in 1980, this seemed to be in tune with what was happening in various ways in English Catholicism: the growth of eucharistic ministers, the replacement of clerical and religious teachers by lay people, the development of informal prayer and house groups, and the presence in many parishes of parish councils made up almost entirely of lay people – a few of them even invading the closely guarded clerical preserve of parish finances. But perhaps the parish council could also be taken as a symbol of what was lacking in this new 'age of the laity'. In too many parishes the setting up of a lay council was a form of tokenism: allowed but hardly encouraged, and in the end given so little responsibility that the true talents of its members were still being undervalued and unused.

At the Cathedral a parish or 'Cathedral Council' had been suggested first in 1966 by the Administrator, Mgr Tomlinson, in response to a letter from Heenan to the clergy encouraging the setting up of parish councils. The idea was to have a council which reflected and 'preserved the diocesan and national status of the Cathedral'; there were to be twelve members elected by the Cathedral congregations and its chapels-of-ease; twelve members representing national Catholic bodies such as the Legion of Mary and the Catenians, and people like the Master of Music and the Cathedral architect to represent specific Cathedral interests. The Cardinal approved the composition, commenting that the diocesan aspect was as important as the parochial one; he did not think, however, that anyone outside London thought that the Cathedral had 'a national aspect'.

In the event, no council was set up until 1969. It was composed of sixteen elected members, thirteen members representing organizations and four priests; it was claired by the Administrator. It had two subcommittees, one for the liturgy, the other for social matters. It was reported that its most noticeable activities had been those of the social subcommittee, first in organizing tea after the High Mass on Sundays, secondly in producing and distributing a fortnightly newsletter. A wry comment in the *News Sheet* in 1970 pointed out that the members were having to face the realities of life as a Cathedral Parish Council, after the heady, honeymoon days of 1969. When they had been asked to discuss First Confession and Communion they found that the only three married members present were so 'senior in wisdom' that they had forgotten all about young children; moreover, the person representing the Union of Catholic Mothers, who might have had some views on the issue, turned out to be a nun![11] There were difficulties of another kind a couple of years later when some members of the council put a proposal that they should be consulted about liturgical changes before they were implemented in the Cathedral – it was not enough, they believed, for these matters to go to their subcommittee. The chairman of the council was the Administrator, Mgr Bartlett; he refused to give such an assurance: no changes were made without consulting the Cardinal, he said, who with the Chapter was responsible for the public worship in the Cathedral. The council still voted by a large majority to support the proposal, but to no avail.[12] The council carried on for a number of years, being re-formed in 1978; one gets the impression that support for it was rather half-hearted. It was finally abolished by a later administrator, Canon Kelly.

Meanwhile, the diocese was being reorganized to provide a number of more manageable areas, each with its own Area Bishop. This was done experimentally in 1976 and then made permanent in 1981. One of the reasons, according to the Cardinal, was 'to involve more people in the life of the Church . . . in the processes of consultation and decision-making which should determine' the pastoral activities of the Area. To help to realize this, all the Areas were to have some form of Pastoral Council or assembly which was to involve laity and clergy in the planning of priorities for action – these Area bodies were thought to be more important than similar bodies at full diocesan level, because the role of the laity in the decision-making process was seen to be fundamental to any pastoral strategy, and was better carried out in smaller units. It was assumed that every parish would have its parish council or equivalent. It appears that by 1988 only two of the five Areas had pastoral councils in the full sense, and the Area which included the Cathedral was not one of them. This failure to accept in practice that the laity had an integral role in planning and decision-making was in line with the disappointing failure to follow up the National Pastoral Congress of 1980 once the euphoria of the moment had passed.[13]

One lay group which was established in these years was the Friends of Westminster Cathedral (1977). It has been very successful, although in a much more traditional lay role – that of raising money for the Cathedral. By 1984 they had donated a total of £256,796 to various Cathedral causes, including two donations from the Friends in the USA to the Choir School Scholarship Fund of over £51,000. In 1986, three bequests from former Friends amounted to over £30,000; this money was invested separately, along with a former bequest, to enable them to respond to requests from the Administrator for occasional financial help. The Friends summarized their aims as, first, to ensure the future of a unique Cathedral building in the centre of London; second, to play a part in the support of a great Christian centre of worship, prayer and ecumenism, and, third, to expand and continue a celebrated tradition of sacred music and liturgy with a world-wide reputation. In practical terms, they aim to give as much financial support as possible and they raise the money and publicize the Cathedral through a wide variety of activities. They have organized flower festivals, concerts, painting competitions and summer fairs; they have established ecumenical links, especially with St Paul's Cathedral; set up an information desk in the Cathedral itself, and published an excellent newsletter twice a year, one of whose features has been a very good series on various aspects of the fabric and decoration of the building.[14] Some of these events have brought visitors in their thousands to the Cathedral, and some of its regular worshippers have complained of the disruption and of the 'non-religious' activities which have become an increasing element in its life. And yet funds have to be raised, and what is the alternative? Regular users of the Cathedral may be glad that the coachloads still do not go to the Cathedral as they do to the Abbey or St Paul's, and that the authorities have been successful in keeping the building free of the commercialism so obtrusive elsewhere: the everyday atmosphere is still that of a house of prayer. But the financial problems are serious, and the solution is beyond the efforts of groups such as the Friends, no matter how dedicated they are.

In a recently published statement (April 1993) the Administrator, Mgr O'Donoghue, described the financial situation as 'bleak but not without promise'. There was an overdraft of nearly a million pounds, and an annual deficit in 1992 of £150,000 (a big improvement on the £350,000 of the previous year). Weekly income from offertory collections and other sources amounted to about £4,200, leaving a shortfall of £3,000. On the expenditure side, salaries for the thirty lay staff and the ten Chaplains came to £350,000; maintenance took £180,000 and the music £145,000. The bleakness is obvious, the promise presumably lies in the halving of the annual deficit through rigid economies and the shedding of full-time staff in areas such as security, cleaning and maintenance.[15] As was said when the great appeal was being planned in the 1970s, the point is soon reached where attempts to cut services and make economies is counter-productive, for the Cathedral is no longer offering enough to satisfy its varied clientele, or is doing so in such a pinch-penny manner as to make it unattractive. The only solution, if the mission of the Cathedral is to grow and develop, is to increase income. As Mgr O'Donoghue put it, people must pray for its mission, make known its requirements and give as generously as they can. In these days, however, it is much easier to get people to give money to support the Cathedral's mission to the poor and homeless than to get them to maintain the building and pay for the everyday services which can so easily be taken for granted.

While Cardinal Hume might have been expected to do everything possible to preserve the musical tradition of the Cathedral and to be concerned about its liturgical development, he surprised a great many people by the way he became so fully involved in a quite different area of pastoral concern. Adrian Hastings has claimed that there was more mature Christian plain speaking in England on social matters in the late 1970s and 1980s than in the previous forty years or so; one might be tempted, in the context of English Catholic church leaders, to make the period a good deal longer than that.[16] All the churches became involved in social issues as moral issues; there was much talk of Liberation Theology in the Third World and of the 'option for the poor' at home, and there were clashes with politicians over the rightful role of the Church in society. Among English Catholics there was a welcome lessening in the primacy of concern which Catholic education had enjoyed for so long and a reduction in the insistence of the demands which it had made on their pockets. There was also a welcome shift of emphasis away from the specifically Catholic charities; not of course that they had not done (and continued to do) invaluable work, but it seemed as though it was now time to adopt a wider perspective and to see social evils as the concern of the Christian citizen, irrespective of the denomination of either victim or helper, and as matters of justice as well as of charity.

The Cardinal's background of the cloister and the élite public school did not give him the first-hand experience of deprivation and other inner-city problems which an active parish priest might have picked up, yet what he has achieved in setting up a network of social agencies around the Cathedral has been remarkable. This practical involvement has been more effective in sensitizing people to the issues than a more outspoken verbal campaign might have been, and has ensured that he is listened to when he speaks to policy makers and public bodies. His concern is for the disadvantaged in the community for which he has a pastoral charge, whether they have any religious affiliation or not. While his involvement has been pivotal he could not have done what has been achieved without the involvement of others, clerical and lay. Part of his role has been to facilitate and, even, to liberate their energies for this work; it has not been all new and much has been built on the devoted work done previously by groups and individuals. The

Cardinal found a particularly useful ally in Mgr Patrick O'Donoghue, Administrator of the Cathedral from 1990 to 1993, who supported the social ventures fully and became involved in them in as practical a way as possible.

The Cardinal was particularly concerned about the number and condition of young homeless people in London. In an attempt to deal with the problem, he set up the Cardinal Hume Centre in 1987. This now runs a number of services, including a hostel for young people between sixteen and twenty years of age. The hostel offers accommodation for up to six months, during which time the young people are encouraged and helped in a number of ways – from re-establishing their self-respect to learning basic life skills. A staff of young volunteers live at the hostel, as does its chaplain, who also serves the next-door church of the Sacred Heart which is a chapel-of-ease of the Cathedral. There is a family centre for young families who live in bed-and-breakfast accommodation around the Victoria area while waiting for proper housing. The centre offers space for mothers and children, together or separate, and a range of counselling and advice services. An evening centre offers similar support to those recently housed, helping with job applications and so on. There is also a charity shop to raise funds towards meeting the annual £250,000 that it takes to run the whole Centre. There are ambitious plans to provide a hostel for young people recovering from substance abuse, a 'drop-in' centre for the young, single homeless and training and education facilities, in partnership with other agencies such as the DePaul Trust and the Westminster Adult Education Institute.[17]

While the Cardinal Hume Centre exists to help young people in need, the Passage Day Centre serves the needs of the older homeless and unemployed. Altogether, the Passage operates twelve 'units' or services and deals with about 300 people each day, working from the old St Vincent's buildings in Carlisle Place. It runs a night shelter (formerly in the Cathedral Hall, now in new but temporary premises in Vauxhall Bridge Road), a clothing store, a laundry and cleaning service, a meals service, a medical surgery, an advice office, a rehabilitation unit, a joint homelessness project (which runs a small hostel for homeless people with mental health problems), a job club, a Probation Service surgery – and a prayer group for the homeless; it is also used by a local housing association as a point of contact. Such a large and professional undertaking could not be kept going by the Cathedral alone, although it was initially a Cathedral project; nowadays it is supported by Westminster Abbey, the Department of the Environment, Westminster City Council, and the London Borough Grants Committee. In addition, in 1993 it received grants from 65 public companies, charitable funds and trusts

– itself witness to the high standing of its work.[18]

The workers in these various projects are a mixture of visiting professionals, volunteers and full-time lay helpers – and religious. The Passage has as its director one of the Sisters of the local community of the Daughters of Charity of St Vincent de Paul, and other members of the same community are also actively involved. The community has been in the parish for many years, engaged in a traditional range of works of mercy and parish visiting, as well as running a hostel for business girls and students and a day care centre for the elderly. They are a link between the older world of Catholic charitable action and the new agencies established by the Cardinal. The same could be said of the lay St Vincent de Paul Society or SVP. For several years its president has been Anthony Bartlett (brother of the former Administrator), who is also the chair of the management committee of the Passage. Here again the new has built on the old and the latter continues to be a worthwhile part of the network of social agencies which now surrounds the Cathedral.

Perhaps it would not be too fanciful to see in these initiatives of the Cardinal a desire to establish a twentieth-century ideal Christian community, not without some debt to the medieval monastic ideal of the house of prayer reaching out into its local community through a range of activities, some spiritual, some material. In this way the liturgy and official prayer of the Cathedral is not something rarified and remote, but the source of an active apostolate, and those who have frequently asked for the Cathedral to be seen to be giving a lead to the rest of the diocese have received a clear response. As the Cardinal put it, 'I say constantly this is where the Church should be, this is our job. Where would St Vincent de Paul have been today? Around Centrepoint.'[19]

While this involvement with the disadvantaged and underprivileged was one form of 'reaching out' to the wider community, another was ecumenism. Without doubt, the 1970s and 1980s were a heyday in England in this respect. From the day of his consecration as Archbishop the Cardinal made it clear that this was to be one of his concerns: in the evening the monks who had taken part in the ceremony at the Cathedral walked to the Abbey and sang Latin Vespers. It could so easily have been a one-off event carried along on the euphoria of the occasion; instead, it seemed to set the tone for the years ahead. In 1981 the Anglican–Roman Catholic International Commission (ARCIC) concluded its long deliberations, and its final report spoke of the two churches having grown closer together 'in faith and charity'. The report was finally accepted by the English Catholic Bishops in

1985. In the meantime, the Pope had made his memorable visit to Canterbury Cathedral, encouraging to all those who were working for closer relations between the Churches and creating an interest in many who had given little thought to ecumenism before. In 1987 the Cardinal made an outstanding contribution to an inter-church gathering at Swanwick when he committed the English Catholic Church to membership of the new body which was to replace the British Council of Churches, spoke of working towards 'organic unity' and stressed that ecumenical progress must build on local initiatives.[20] Since then the temperature has cooled in the face of Rome's lack of enthusiasm for ARCIC and its outright opposition to the Church of England's decision over the ordination of women. But not all the gains were lost, and the Cathedral is itself a witness that the Cardinal's 'local initiatives' are being pursued.

In April 1993, the Administrator, Mgr O'Donoghue, wrote that the 'mission' of the Cathedral reached out beyond the building to other Christian churches. The *Bulletin* for January 1994 gave one indication of what this could mean in practice. The issue marked the annual Week of Prayer for Christian Unity and contained a 'Thought for Unity Week' from the Bishop of London, an article by a local vicar and an editorial on the question of unity. This admitted that some people might be losing heart: the road to unity was a hard and winding one, and at times it was easy to become tired and even suspicious of others on the road; but we must, according to the writer, continue to listen to and learn from 'our travelling companions' from the other churches who might be using their God-given gifts more fruitfully than we were. The writer then listed the main inter-church events planned for the week in the Cathedral. The clergy and choir of St Paul's Cathedral were to sing Evensong, to replace the normal Vespers; the next day there would be a Mass according to one of the Eastern rite liturgies. On the Sunday, the Cathedral Administrator was to preach in Westminster Abbey, while the leader of the Orthodox Church in Britain would preach in the Cathedral. Later on that day clergy and people from the 35 member churches of Westminster Christian Council were to attend Solemn Vespers in the Cathedral, and the Dean of St Paul's was to preach; the choir would be joined by that from the Methodist Central Hall and the Russian Orthodox Cathedral. Finally, the Cathedral clergy and choir would be singing Solemn Vespers at St Paul's the next day. That none of this appears revolutionary or likely to cause protest shows how far things have moved since the 1960s with its cautious keeping of the 'Chair of Union Octave'.

In addition to its liturgical function and its pastoral-cum-social mission, there remains one final element of the Cathedral to be looked at – its position as a national centre or shrine for English Catholicism. As we have seen, this ideal was part of Vaughan's original inspiration, and it has featured over the years in different ways, resurfacing from time to time usually as an argument for or against a particular course of action. On a very limited number of occasions the Cathedral has truly been the centre of English Catholic attention – the Eucharistic Congress of 1908 and the Papal visit of 1982 are the most obvious examples. The coming of television has made some difference, of course, with services broadcast from the Cathedral – a Service of Readings on Good Friday morning, a Christmas Midnight Mass, and so on. In addition, the more relaxed attitude to holding concerts in the Cathedral has allowed the building to be seen more frequently on national television. But all this is largely peripheral. It is difficult enough to promote the Cathedral as the centre for the diocese, given the contemporary stress on forming smaller community units and the breaking up of the diocese into pastoral areas; and perhaps parish priests do not take kindly to appeals for their people to attend numerous functions at the Cathedral. It is a centre for annual get-togethers for Catholic societies such as the Union of Catholic Mothers, the Scouts and the Catenians, and there are annual Masses for nurses and for members of the legal profession, but even these are more likely to be attended by members from London, or at most, the Home Counties. Cardinal Heenan's judgement that only people in London thought the Cathedral had a national role was typically blunt but realistic.

And yet, it may be that it has got a national function to perform. Just as the Cardinal is taken to be the head and spokesman for the Catholic Church in England, called upon for comment and listened to with respect, so the Cathedral may be taken as its flagship, sometimes, perhaps, looked at with more curiosity than understanding, but able to impress with its reverence and splendour.

NOTES

1 AAW, Boxfile 'Cathedral', document by Mgr P. O'Donoghue.
2 *Bulletin* (June 1985).
3 See A. Atha and S. Drummond, *The Good Schools Guide, 1989*.
4 *Bulletin* (June 1985).
5 *The Independent* (11 October 1992).
6 Cathedral *News Sheet* (February 1971).
7 BBC interview (19 August 1992?)

8   See recent Cathedral *Bulletins* for details.
9   *Westminster Diocesan Year Books*; A. Hastings, *A History of English Christianity 1920–1985* (1987), pp. 603, 630.
10   *The Tablet* (5 June 1982); *Friends Newsletter* (October 1984); *The Pope in Britain* (St Paul's Publications, 1982), pp. 5–6, 106.
11   AAW, He 3/52–54: Tomlinson/Heenan letters (December 1966); Report on Parish Councils (May 1970); *News Sheet* (July 1970).
12   AAW, He 3/52–54, Parish Council Minutes (10 January 1972).
13   *Westminster Diocesan Year Book* (1982 and 1986); quotations from 'Planning for the Spirit' (1976) in 1982 *Year Book*.
14   *Friends Newsletters*.
15   Cathedral *Bulletin* (April 1993).
16   Hastings, p. 658.
17   *Bulletin* (February 1993): S. Cullen, Director of Centre.
18   Annual Report (1993).
19   Quoted in P. Stanford, *Cardinal Hume and the Changing Face of English Catholicism* (1993), p. 99. Centrepoint is a major hostel for the homeless in central London.
20   The 'Swanwick Declaration' (September 1987): see *The Times* (5 September 1987), pp. 4, 8.

Conclusion

A lasting vision

Westminster Cathedral is a symbol and instrument of faith in Christ. It proclaims his presence in the life of our nation, diocese and parish community, and creates and sustains our Christian way of life. This it does through the Sacraments, liturgy and worship, by being a place of prayer and recollection, by being a centre of excellence, and by responding to the call of Christ to show his love in action among those most in need.

THE ABOVE IS THE MISSION STATEMENT of the Cathedral today. Would it have received Cardinal Vaughan's approval? He certainly saw the Cathedral as a symbol of faith in Christ which would proclaim him to nation, diocese and parish. He would also have agreed that it was a source of grace, giving Christian life to those who worshipped and received the sacraments in it. He would probably have been surprised to see that liturgy and worship were not given pride of place, and in particular that no mention was made of the daily performance of the Divine Office. He would have given his full support to the 'centre of excellence' ideal, and might have added that it should also be a model for others to follow with regard to ceremonial and music. If he had been asked to comment on the final phrase, he would have understood 'those most in need' to refer to those whose spiritual needs were pressing for pastoral attention and not to those in material or social want. Presumably he would not have noticed the absence of any reference to relations with other churches, an omission which might look strange to the modern reader.

All this is, of course, merely supposition. When Cardinal Hume was interviewed about how he saw the Cathedral today,[1] he started by taking an imaginary walk around its outside. There is the Clergy House in Francis Street and also the Catholic Central Library; moving down Carlisle Place, one comes to the Sisters, 'so very much part of this place', and then The

Passage, 'a marvellous place', feeding and caring for 300 people every day and with a very high reputation in official circles such as the Department for the Environment. Turning towards the front of the Cathedral one sees the Cathedral Bookshop, and then, in Ambrosden Avenue, the Cathedral Hall, used by so many different groups and until recently the home of the Night Shelter; finally, there is the entrance to the Choir School. Further afield, in Osborne Street, is the Cardinal Hume Centre. All these things are connected with the Cathedral and take its message out to a wider community.

Inside the Cathedral, the Cardinal believes that the most striking feature is the sense of the building being a house of prayer – there are always people there, attending the services, praying quietly on their own, waiting for confession . . . 'if ever we lose that, we're finished'; if the Cathedral were ever to become a mere tourist attraction, or a house of beautiful art treasures, it would have lost what is fundamental to the Catholic faith. With the services and prayer inside the building, and the work that reaches out from it to the local community, the two great commandments of loving God and loving one's neighbour can be seen as part of the life of the Cathedral.

Relating to this, the Cardinal believes, is the necessity to ensure that people feel at home in the Cathedral and regard it as belonging to them. There is a danger, especially in a large diocese, that people in the parishes think of the Cathedral as far away, not connected with them and so not meeting their needs. It is, obviously, to their local parish church that people should feel attracted in the first place and the decentralization to the pastoral areas is part of creating smaller units which people can relate to more easily. The danger here is that people lose the sense of the cohesion of the diocese – while decentralization must take place, there is still a need for a focal point for the whole diocese; after all, the Area Bishops and the parishes are acting in the name of the Bishop. One of the most important events in the year from this point of view is the Chrism Mass in Holy Week when all the clergy from the diocese are invited to concelebrate with the Cardinal – a recognition liturgically that all are one. Another event that helps to create a sense of belonging is the gathering of five or six hundred adults from parishes around the diocese on the first Sunday in Lent, as part of the Rite of Christian Initiation of Adults – 'a precious moment'. The Cathedral has some great moments in the liturgical year – Good Friday afternoon, the Easter Vigil, Easter Sunday morning – and, of course, Christmas Midnight Mass. There will always be a tension between those forces which pull people towards the centre and those which attract them away towards their own locality;

perhaps not enough is done to bring people into the Cathedral throughout the year.

On the question of the artistic side of the Cathedral, the Cardinal is convinced that it is important to be 'guided by the Bentley vision but not gagged by it', and to listen to the Arts Advisory Committee and the experts. The Cathedral has, he believes, a special character given to it by the stark contrasts between the colours of the marbles and the mosaics, and the gaunt, uncovered brickwork.

A hundred years of the Cathedral's history cannot be summed up in a few lines, but something of the lasting achievement of its founder is captured in Cardinal Hume's words:

> A wonderful place, a house of prayer, able to switch from one role to another without any difficulty – there are national events, special occasions for the diocese and then there are parish events. But the pride of the Cathedral is the way in which it draws people to pray and to receive the Sacraments.

NOTE

1   Author's interview with Cardinal Hume (21 January 1994).

Appendix 1

The Cathedral Cardinals

Herbert Vaughan	April 1892 – June 1903
Francis Bourne	September 1903 – January 1935
Arthur Hinsley	March 1935 – March 1943
Bernard Griffin	December 1943 – August 1956
William Godfrey	December 1956 – January 1963
John Carmel Heenan	September 1963 – November 1975
George Basil Hume	March 1976 –

Cathedral Administrators

Mgr P. Fenton	1895(?)–1904
Mgr Moyes	1904–1905
Mgr M. Howlett	1905–1947
Mgr C. Collingwood	1947–1954
Mgr G. Wheeler	1954–1964
Mgr G. A. Tomlinson	1964–1967
Mgr F. Bartlett	1967–1977
Mgr O. Kelly	1977–1989
Mgr P. O'Donoghue	1989–1993
Mgr G. Stack	1993–

Appendix 2

Inscription on the Foundation stone

Latin text, opposite, and translation, below.

On the 29th day of June in the year 1895, the eighteenth year of the Pontificate of POPE LEO XIII. and the fifty-ninth year of the Reign of QUEEN VICTORIA, on the Feast of the HOLY APOSTLES PETER AND PAUL, the anniversary of the day on which, two years before, England was solemnly consecrated to the MOST BLESSED VIRGIN MARY and to SAINT PETER, this FIRST STONE OF WESTMINSTER CATHEDRAL,—to be dedicated to our LORD JESUS CHRIST, WHO REDEEMED US BY HIS MOST PRECIOUS BLOOD, to the MOST BLESSED VIRGIN MARY HIS IMMACULATE MOTHER, and the APOSTLE SAINT PETER HIS FIRST VICAR, to SAINT JOSEPH Patron of the Catholic Church and of the interior life, and, as secondary Patrons, to SAINT AUGUSTINE Apostle of England and all Saints of Great Britain, and to SAINT PATRICK and the other Saints of Ireland,—was laid, according to the Rite of the Holy Roman Church, by His Eminence HERBERT CARDINAL VAUGHAN, THIRD ARCHBISHOP OF WESTMINSTER, with the gracious assistance of His Eminence MICHAEL CARDINAL LOGUE, ARCHBISHOP OF ARMAGH AND PRIMATE OF ALL IRELAND, in the presence of many Bishops, and of a vast multitude of the Clergy and of the Faithful and others.

JESUS, our MOST LOVING REDEEMER, have mercy on England.

HOLY MARY, MOTHER OF GOD, whose Dowry is England; SAINT PETER, Patron of England; SAINT JOSEPH, Spouse of the Most Blessed Virgin Mary; and all Saints of Great Britain and Ireland,—pray for England.

DIE XXIX JUNII ANNO MDCCCXCV,

PONTIFICATUS LEONIS PAPAE XIII ANNO DECIMO OCTAVO
REGNI VICTORIAE REGINAE QUINQUAGESIMO NONO,
IN FESTO SANCTORUM APOSTOLORUM PETRI ET PAULI,

DIE ANNIVERSARIA QUA DUOBUS ANTE ANNIS
BEATISSIMAE MARIAE VIRGINI ET SANCTO PETRO
ANGLIA SOLEMNITER CONSECRATA FUIT,

HIC LAPIS PRIMARIUS

ECCLESIAE CATHEDRALIS WESTMONASTERIENSIS,

DOMINO NOSTRO JESU CHRISTO

QUI PRETIOSISSIMO SUO SANGUINE NOS REDEMIT,
BEATISSIMAE MARIAE VIRGINI IMMACULATAE EJUS MATRI
SANCTOQUE PETRO APOSTOLO, PRIMO EJUS VICARIO,
SANCTO JOSEPH ECCLESIAE CATHOLICAE VITAEQUE INTERIORIS PATRONO,

AC DEINDE

SANCTO AUGUSTINO ANGLIAE APOSTOLO OMNIBUSQUE SANCTIS BRITANNIAE,
SANCTO PATRITIO ALIISQUE HIBERNIAE SANCTIS

DEDICANDAE,

AB EMO. ET RMO. DNO. HERBERTO CARDINALI VAUGHAN
ARCHIEPISCOPO WESTMONASTERIENSI TERTIO,

EMO. ET RMO. DNO. MICHAELE CARDINALI LOGUE
ARCHIEPISCOPO ARMACANO TOTIUSQUE HIBERNIAE PRIMATE
BENIGNE ASSISTENTE,

EPISCOPIS PLURIMIS CUM INGENTI ECCLESIASTICORUM,
FIDELIUM ALIORUMQUE MULTITUDINE CIRCUMSTANTIBUS,

JUXTA SANCTAE ROMANAE ECCLESIAE RITUM
POSITUS EST.

JESU, AMANTISSIME REDEMPTOR NOSTER,
MISERERE ANGLIAE.

SANCTA MARIA MATER DEI, CUJUS DOS EST ANGLIA NOSTRA,
SANCTE PETRE, ANGLIAE PATRONE,
SANCTE JOSEPH BEATISSIMAE MARIAE VIRGINIS SPONSE,
OMNESQUE SANCTI BRITANNIAE ET HIBERNIAE,
ORATE PRO ANGLIA.

Bibliography

The following are the main printed works consulted or referred to in the notes.

H. Andrews, *Westminster Retrospect: A Memoir of Sir Richard Terry* (Oxford, 1948)

G. A. Beck (ed.), *The English Catholics 1850–1950* (1950)

Benedictines of Stanbrook, *In a Great Tradition* (1956)

Bergh, Abbot, *The Book of the Consecration of the Cathedral* (1910)

C. Binfield, 'A chapel and its architect: James Cubitt and Union Chapel, Islington 1874–1889' in D. Wood (ed.), *The Church and the Arts: Studies in Church History*, vol. 28 (Oxford, 1992)

G. Bovini, *Ravenna Mosaics* (1957)

O. Chadwick, *The Victorian Church* (2 vols; 2nd edn, 1972)

R. Currie, A. Gilbert and L. Horsley, *Churches and Churchgoers* (Oxford, 1977)

T. Day, *A Discography of Tudor Church Music* (1989)

W. de l'Hopital, *Westminster Cathedral and Its Architect* (2 vols, n.d., but 1919)

R. J. Dingle, *Cardinal Bourne at Westminster* (1934)

R. Dixon and S. Muthesius, *Victorian Architecture* (1978)

B. Fletcher, *A History of Architecture on the Comparative Method* (16th edn, 1956)

E. Gill, *Autobiography* (1940)

A. Hastings, *A History of English Christianity 1920–1985* (1987)

L. Hollen Lees, *Exiles of Erin* (Manchester, 1979)

J. D. Holmes, *More Roman Than Rome* (1978)

P. Howell, 'Letters from J. F. Bentley to Charles Hadfield', *Architectural History: Journal of the Society of Architectural Historians of Great Britain*, vol. 23 (1980) and vol. 25 (1982)

S. Jervis, *Penguin Dictionary of Design and Designers* (1984)

R. Kollar, *Westminster Cathedral: From Dream to Reality* (Edinburgh, 1987)

R. Krautheimer, *Early Christian and Byzantine Architecture* (1965)

S. Leslie (ed.), *Letters of Herbert Cardinal Vaughan to Lady Herbert of Lea, 1867–1903* (1942)

W. R. Lethaby (ed.), *Ernest Gimson, His Life and Work* (London/ Stratford/Oxford, 1924)

B. Little, *Catholic Churches Since 1623* (1966)

A. McCormack, *Cardinal Vaughan* (1966)

H. McLeod, *Class and Religion in the Late Victorian City* (1974)

D. Mathew, *Catholicism in England* (1936)

T. Moloney, *Westminster, Whitehall and the Vatican: The Role of Cardinal Hinsley 1935–1943* (1985)

E. R. Norman, *The English Catholic Church in the 19th Century* (1989)

E. Oldmeadow, *Francis Cardinal Bourne* (2 vols, 1940, 1944)

N. Pevsner, *The Buildings of England: London* 1: *The Cities of London and Westminster* (3rd edn, 1973)

N. Pevsner, *An Outline of European Architecture* (7th edn, 1964)

E. S. Purcell, *Life of Cardinal Manning, Archbishop of Westminster* (2 vols, 1895)

C. H. Reilly, *Some Architectural Problems of Today* (Liverpool and London, 1924)

A. Robertson, *More Than Music* (1961)

A. Saint, *Richard Norman Shaw* (1976)

W. W. Scott-Moncrieff, *John Francis Bentley* (1924)

J. G. Snead-Cox, *The Life of Cardinal Vaughan* (2 vols, 1912)

G. Stamp, *Robert Weir Schultz, Architect, and His Work for the Marquess of Bute* (Mount Stewart, 1981)

G. Stamp and C. Amery, *Victorian Buildings of London* (1980)

P. Stanford, *Cardinal Hume and the Changing Face of English Catholicism* (1993)

J. N. Tarn, 'Liverpool's two cathedrals' in D. Wood (ed.), *The Church and the Arts: Studies in Church History*, vol. 28 (Oxford, 1992)

R. Terry, *Catholic Church Music* (1907)

R. Terry, *The Music of the Roman Rite: A Manual for Choirmasters* (1931)

M. Walsh, *The Tablet 1840–1900: A Commemorative History* (1990)

G. Wheeler, *In Truth and Love* (Leeds, 1990)

M. Yorke, *Eric Gill, Man of Flesh and Spirit* (1981)

Index